BORN UNWANTED
Developmental Effects
of Denied Abortion

PREVIOUS MONOGRAPHS PUBLISHED UNDER
THE AUSPICES OF THE TRANSNATIONAL FAMILY
RESEARCH INSTITUTE

David, H. P. *Family planning and abortion in the socialist countries of Central and Eastern Europe.* New York: The Population Council, 1970.

David, H. P. (Ed.). *Abortion research: International experience.* Lexington, Mass.: Heath, 1974.

van der Tak, J. *Abortion, fertility, and changing legislation: An international review.* Lexington, Mass.: Heath, 1974.

David, H. P., and Cambiaso, S. (Org.). *Epidemiology of abortion and practices of fertility regulation in Latin America: Selected reports.* Washington: Pan American Health Organization, 1975.

David, H. P., Friedman, H. L., van der Tak, J., and Sevilla, M. J. (Eds.). *Abortion in psychosocial perspective: Trends in transnational research.* New York: Springer, 1978.

David, H. P., and McIntyre, R. J. *Reproductive behavior: Central and Eastern European experience.* New York: Springer, 1981.

BORN UNWANTED:

Developmental Effects
of Denied Abortion

Editors: *Henry P. DAVID,* Ph.D.
Transnational Family Research Institute, Bethesda, Md.

Zdeněk DYTRYCH, M.D., C.Sc.
Psychiatric Research Institute, Prague

Zdeněk MATĚJČEK, Ph.D., C.Sc.
Postgraduate Medical Institute, Prague

Vratislav SCHÜLLER, Ph.D., C.Sc.
Psychiatric Research Institute, Prague

SPRINGER PUBLISHING COMPANY/NEW YORK
AVICENUM, CZECHOSLOVAK MEDICAL
PRESS/PRAGUE
1988

ABOUT THE CO-EDITORS

Henry P. DAVID, Ph.D., is a clinical psychologist, Director of the Transnational Family Research Institute, Bethesda, Maryland, and Associate Clinical Professor of Psychology, Department of Psychiatry, University of Maryland Medical School, Baltimore. He has participated in cooperative research projects on reproductive behavior with colleagues in more than 20 countries, published extensively, and is a frequent consultant to international organizations.

Zdeněk DYTRYCH, M.D., C.Sc., is a senior research psychiatrist at the Psychiatric Research Institute, Prague, and head of the PRI psychosocial family research group.

Zdeněk MATĚJČEK, Ph.D., C.Sc., is a child psychologist on the teaching staff of the Department of Pediatrics, Postgraduate Medical Institute, Prague, and Associate Professor of Clinical Psychology, Charles University. He is the author and co-author of several books on child psychology, including "Psychological Deprivation in Childhood" (together with *J. Langmeier*), which has been published in Czech, English, German, and Russian.

Vratislav SCHÜLLER, Ph.D., C.Sc., is a senior research sociologist at the Psychiatric Research Institute, Prague, specializing in psychosocial family research studies for over 20 years.

Library of Congress Cataloging-in-Publication Data

Born unwanted.

Bibliography: p.
Includes index.
1. Abortion--Psychological aspects--Longitudinal studies. 2. Abortion--Social aspects--Longitudinal studies. 3. Child development--Longitudinal studies. I. David, Henry Philip, 1923-   . [DNLM: 1. Child Development. 2. Child, Unwanted--psychology. 3. Follow-Up Studies. WS 105 B736]
HQ767.B59 1988   363.4'6   88-16651
ISBN 0-8261-6080-8

© Transnational Family Research Institute, 1988
Springer Publishing Company, Inc., 536 Broadway, New York, NY 10012-3955 (U.S.A.) has the sole distribution rights for all countries with the exception of the socialist countries.

Contents

obviously these authors never heard of adoption!

5

Preface

*I dream about the day when all children
born are welcome and when sexuality is an
expression of joy and caring.* *)
Elise Ottesen-Jensen

The above statement by the distinguished Swedish pioneer of family planning provides an apt perspective for our cooperative studies of the developmental effects of denied abortion on children to whom women gave birth involuntarily. Although there has been much discussion of the dynamics of intended and unintended conceptions, and wanted and unwanted pregnancies and childrearing, it has seldom been possible to conduct follow-up studies of children born unwanted from childhood to early adulthood. Most often, prevailing legislation and/or the absence of national population registers render very unlikely even the prospect of organizing follow-up or pair-matched control studies of such children.

Unusual conditions existing in Sweden facilitated conducting the first longitudinal study of children born in 1939-42 to women denied therapeutic abortion. The Swedish psychiatrist, Dr. *Hans Forssman,* and his social worker colleague, Dr. *Inga Thuwe,* followed these children through the Swedish registers for 35 years. We are very pleased to have a summary report of their pioneering research prepared especially for this monograph. It was their initiative which stimulated the study of children born in 1961-63 to Prague women twice denied abortion for the same pregnancy and pair-matched controls. To the best of our knowledge, the Prague study is unique in its design and methodology. The Northern Finland studies of children deemed unwanted by their mothers during the late stages of gestation were initiated in 1966 by Dr. *Paula Rantakallio,* Professor of Public Health Science at the University of Oulu. Subsequent pair-matched follow-up inquiries were conducted by *Antero Myhrman,* using some of the procedures tested in Prague. His contribution is an important addition to this monograph.

Numerous colleagues and organizations have supported our Prague efforts over the years, most importantly the former and current directors of the Psychiatric Research Institute, Prof. *L. Hanzlíček* and Doc. *J. Gebhart,* and of the Postgraduate Medical Institute, Department of Pediatrics, Prof. *J. Švejcar* and Prof. *J. Dunovský.* The study would not have been possible without the initiative and collaboration of

---

*) Cited in *Why is it so difficult with abortion?,* published by the Swedish Board of Health and Welfare, Stockholm, 1982.

Dr. *E. Stupková*, Director of Prague Public Health Services, when our efforts were in the beginning stages. Similarly, Dr. *V. Fischelová* assisted significantly in the organizational phase and in conducting the first wave of interviews.

As Czech and American researchers we are pleased to acknowledge the continuing encouragement of national and international organizations. The series of investigations reported from Prague were supported in part at various times by grants from the Center for Population Research of the U.S. National Institute of Child Health and Human Development (HD-05569) and the Ford Foundation to the Transnational Family Research Institute, by the Human Reproduction Division of the World Health Organization to the Psychiatric Research Institute, and by the Czechoslovak State Research Plan to the Postgraduate Medical Institute and the Psychiatric Research Institute. The most recent follow-up was supported entirely by the Czechoslovak State Research Plan. The Transnational Family Research Institute made a small contribution to the preparation of this monograph, which is a joint Czechoslovak - U.S. publication. The World Federation for Mental Health and its Committee on Responsible Parenthood have actively sponsored or co-sponsored some of the more than 50 presentations at scientific meetings and are also providing the international auspices under which the monograph is published.

We are most grateful to the many friends and colleagues who have assisted our endeavors over the past nearly 20 years. Regretfully, it is impossible to list all the names. It is particularly appropriate, however, to express our appreciation for the support of colleagues at the World Health Organization, Drs. *Mark Belsey, Herbert L. Friedman*, and *Alexander Kessler*, the methodological guidance given by Dr. *Luděk Kubička* of the Psychiatric Research Institute; the extensive data processing assistance provided by Ing. *Z. Roth*, Ing. *Z. Holoubková*, and Ing. *V. Hynčica* of the Mathematical Department, Institute for Hygiene and Epidemiology, Prague, and *Raymond L. Johnson* of the Transnational Family Research Institute (Bethesda); and for the stimulating discussions of ideas over many years with *Warren B. Miller* (Transnational Family Research Institute, Palo Alto).

Working cross-culturally across linguistic and other barriers is never an easy task. We are most grateful to our understanding translator, *Aleš Klégr*, Ph.D., to our colleague and editor, *Jean van der Tak*, to the editorial and production team at Avicenum, Czechoslovak Medical Press, to *Ursula Springer* and *Barbara Watkins* at Springer Publishing Co., to *Ann Rosendall* at the Transnational Family Research Institute, and especially to *Karla Topičová* (Psychiatric Research Institute), social worker and technical assistant, who has been collaborating with us from the very beginning and whose persistent interest, steadfast dedication, and organizational talents transformed the Prague study from an idea to reality. We are pleased to share our experience with colleagues everywhere.

Henry P. David

Prague, Czechoslovakia *Zdeněk Dytrych*
Bethesda, Maryland, USA *Zdeněk Matějček*
May 1987 *Vratislav Schüller*

8

Chapter 1

Overview: A Brief History of Abortion and Studies of Denied Abortion

Henry P. David

Induced abortion is one of the oldest and most controversial forms of fertility regulation. No other elective surgical procedure has evoked as much world-wide debate, generated such emotional and moral controversy, or received greater sustained attention from the public and the media. While considerable data have accumulated about social, demographic, epidemiological and health aspects of abortion, very little is known about the longitudinal development of children to whom women gave birth involuntarily following denial of request for legal abortion or when abortion was not a legally available option (e.g., *Tietze* and *Henshaw*, 1986).

Sociocultural ambivalence, political sensitivities and methodological barriers continue to inhibit abortion-related social science research in the United States and most other countries. For example, during 38 days of testimony before the Select Committee on Population of the U.S. House of Representatives in 1978, more than 150 specialists from the U.S.A. and abroad were invited to testify on topics ranging from the reliability of demographic data to the safety of modern methods of contraception, and from problems of teenage pregnancy to the impact of an aging population. By the time of its dissolution in March 1979, the Committee had issued 11 volumes of hearings and six reports containing 133 recommendations for legislative or administrative action. Elective abortion was never mentioned. In accord with prior agreement, each session chairperson had forewarned every witness not to talk about abortion and threatened to cut off promptly anyone who tried to discuss this sensitive topic (*David*, 1980). In late 1986, with another political party represented in the White House, a great deal of pressure was exerted not to provide government research funds for testing and evaluating the contragestive pill RU 486 (mifepristone) which holds the promise of eventually becoming a safe self-administered menses inducer in the first four to five weeks of amenorrhea (*Couzinet et al.*, 1986).

This monograph reviews and discusses the limited knowledge on the developmental effects of denied abortion from childhood through adolescence to early adulthood. Available studies come from Czechoslovakia, Finland, and Sweden. Major focus is on the Prague cohort which follows the development of 220 children born in 1961-63 to women twice denied abortion for the same pregnancy and pair-matched controls from age nine through ages 21-23.

9

To set the stage, this chapter summarizes the history of abortion and the legal constraints gradually placed on its practice in the United States and other countries; the eventual liberalization of legislation, beginning in 1920 in the Soviet Union and currently covering about 76 percent of the world's population; and the initial efforts to conduct research on the developmental effects of denied abortion.

It is the major thesis of the monograph that an unwanted pregnancy, operationally defined as actively rejected by the woman reasonably early in gestation, leads, in the aggregate, to a social environment conducive to slightly deviant development in childhood and evolving into gradually worsening social difficulties and problems in adolescence and early adulthood, when compared to the social development of children born to women who accepted their pregnancy and did not request abortion.

Subsequent chapters consider unwantedness in demographic and psychological perspective, in terms of the wantedness-unwantedness continuum, and in relation to responsible parenthood. The Göteborg, Prague, and Northern Finland cohorts are presented in greater detail along with related Swedish studies. The last chapter considers questions frequently raised by interested colleagues, our responses and conclusions, and suggestions for future research and educational policies designed to reduce the incidence of unwanted pregnancies.

Early History of Abortion

The oldest known medical texts citing abortion techniques appeared in China around 2737 B.C., more than 4,700 years ago (*Taussig*, 1936). There was no condemnation of abortion in classical antiquity. The ancient Greeks advocated abortion to regulate population size and maintain stable social and economic conditions. Plato (400 B.C.) recommended abortion for a pregnant women over 40 years of age (or if her mate was over 50) and viewed termination of unwanted pregnancy as a means of perfecting the body politic. Aristotle also suggested abortion to limit family size. Hippocrates spoke against abortion for medical reasons, fearing injury to the woman, but recommended it on occasion by prescribing violent exercises.

The term "abortion," as presently used, stems from the Latin "aboriri," meaning "to perish" (*Millar*, 1934). In Rome and throughout most of the Roman Empire's existence, there were few if any legal restrictions on abortion. The prevailing opinion was that the fetus was part of the woman's body and that she could request its removal.

With the fall of the Roman Empire and the rise of Christianity, the world gradually moved into the period later described as the Dark Ages, followed by the Middle Ages. During these times, nearly every aspect of fertility regulation was managed by women, usually without the aid of men or the medical professions. That midwives procured abortions clandestinely is apparent from the references to severe penalties imposed for the practice of inserting stems into pregnant uteri (*Davis*, 1974).

10

Western Religions

The ancient Hebrews had a term for abortion, "neftel," meaning "dropping out," but it is not mentioned in the Old or New Testaments. The early Christians, following Judaic views, condemned abortion but did not view on abortion "before the soul is in the body" as murder (*Callahan*, 1970). While there had been discussion in the Catholic Church about when life begins, this was more important in the theoretical than in the practical order (*David*, 1980). In 1869, Pope Pius IX, in his Constitution *Apostolicae Sedis*, "made a sharp change in church law by eliminating any distinction between a formed and unformed fetus in meting out the penalty of excommunication for abortion," even to save the life of the woman. Therapeutic abortion on medical indication was not explicitly and publicly condemned by any Roman Catholic authority before 1895 (*Means*, 1970).

An extensive examination of statements by western religious scholars of diverse persuasions led *Moore* (1974) to the conclusion that "no major religion, with the possible exception of Roman Catholicism, has a unified position on the matter of induced abortion." There are varying interpretations among the major religions and within particular sects of the definition of "person" and of the time at which an individual human life begins. Representatives for a variety of positions can be found in each of the major religions: some religious bodies have changed or altered their positions over the centuries or in recent years, rather than maintaining a single unbroken history of opposition or support.

Non-Western Beliefs

In the non-Western world, abortion prohibitions were not part of the indigenous cultural, religious, philosophical, and legal traditions but "products of imperialism or the wave of westernization attendant upon the Industrial Revolution" (*Lee*, 1973, p. 348). In ancient China, for example, abortion was perceived more as "parents' self-inflicted punishment" than a sin against God or a crime against society; traditional Chinese penal codes did not include any provisions for abortion. It was not until the late Manchu dynasty during the end of the 19th century that abortion was prohibited. This action was motivated not so much by conviction as by desire to "modernize" the Chinese legal system, one of the conditions for removing the extraterritorial regime imposed by the Western powers.

In Japan, abortion was not considered a crime until the Meiji Reform modernized the judiciary. A Penal Code was adopted, patterned after the French model with its antiabortion provisions. Since the French religious view of God as the creator of life was alien to the Confucian philosophy then prevailing in much of Japan, sanctions against abortion were rarely enforced.

Islam's view on abortion is not precise. While abortion is strictly prohibited after the fetus has acquired a life or soul of its own, there is disagreement on when the soul enters the fetus. Most scholars concur that entry of the soul probably does not occur until the fetus assumes human shape, estimated at between 40 and 120 days (*Omran*, 1972).

Condemnation of the practice of abortion can be found in the sacred literature of the East, including Hinduism, Taoism, and Buddhism. In actual practice, Buddhism is more of a philosophy and its practitioners tend to separate religion and reality. In Thailand, for example, it is frequently held that it is better to commit a small sin to prevent a bigger future sin; Gautama Buddha's saying that "many birds cause suffering" has been rephrased as "many children make you poor."

While there are considerable differences in the views of abortion presented by diverse religious scholars, both Western and non-Western, distinctions must be made between official, semi-official, and nonofficial religious attitudes and actual behaviors as perceived within the sociocultural context of a given time. Some flexibility can be found almost everywhere and even the strictest prohibitions are seldom fully enforced.

Legal Restraints

From 1307 to 1803 in England, and from 1607 to 1828 in the American colonies and the United States, common law allowed women abortion at will (*Means*, 1971; *Mohr*, 1978). Under common law (that body of legal rules derived from decisions of judges based upon accepted customs and traditions), abortion was not considered an offense if performed with the woman's consent before she was "quick with child." (Quickening marked the time when the first movements of the fetus were felt by the woman, usually around the 16th to 18th week of gestation.) Even if performed after quickening, the offense was usually considered only a misdemeanor.

In 1803 in England, during the reign of George III, Lord Ellenborough's Act made procurement of an abortion before quickening a felony "to be punished by fine, imprisonment, or exposure in the pillory, or that the criminal may be publicly or privately whipped or transported beyond the sea for any term not exceeding 14 years" (*Hodge*, 1869). Procuring an abortion after quickening was considered murder, punishable by death. The Act was modified under George IV and supplanted, during Queen Victoria's reign, by the Offences Against the Person Act of 1861, which decreed surgical abortion at any state of pregnancy a criminal offense, punishable by life imprisonment (*Dickens*, 1966).

During the latter part of the 19th century, European views on the restrictions of abortion were spread by the Colonial Powers throughout Africa and Asia. The strict prohibitions of Spain are refrected in many statutes promulgated in South America. In numerous countries of Asia and Africa, restrictions remained in force after independence had been gained, and were continued even after the departing Colonial Power had liberalized its own statutes.

12

United States

The first law dealing specifically with the legal status of abortion in the United States was passed in 1821 by the General Assembly of Connecticut. It restricted the administration of a "noxious or destructive substance . . . to any woman then quick with child" (*Connecticut,* 1821). Surgical abortion before quickening was first prohibited by a section of the New York Revised Statutes of 1829 (enacted in 1828), which also contained an express therapeutic exception, justifying abortion "if necessary to preserve the life of the mother" (*Means,* 1968).

A review of documents contemporary with the passage of the New York State legislation suggests that the primary concern at the time was not with the unquickened fetus but with protecting the life and health of women with unwanted pregnancies from damage by abortion (*Means,* 1970). This was the pre-Lister era of medicine when every operation entailed the possibility of life-threatening infection (*Lister,* 1867). In some hospitals, one operation in every three ended in death. The emphasis of the New York legislators on preventing unnecessary surgery is reflected in their decision to place the abortion statute in the Penal Code instead of the Medical Practices Act.

By 1850, eleven more American states had followed the lead of New York. Only in New Jersey did one of the statutes receive a judicial construction by a contemporary court, explaining why the legislation had been passed: "The design of the statute was not to prevent the procuring of abortions so much as to guard the health and life of the mother against the consequences of such attempts" (cited by *Means,* 1970, p. 140).

Perhaps it was the temper of the times that persuaded the New York legislators in 1828, and their colleagues in other states, to place the abortion statutes in the Penal Code instead of in the medical practices or ethics acts where every previous and subsequent law governing medical and surgical procedures is to be found. The reasoning seems to have been that in all other operations a combination of a patient's natural caution and the practitioner's conscience sufficed to prevent unnecessary surgery. Only in the case of abortion did legislators add restrictive provisions to the penal codes.

The ineffectiveness of the 19th century abortion sanctions in the United States is apparent from public records (*Nebinger,* 1870; *Gordon,* 1976). Despite the new laws, abortionists were operating publicly and being acquitted by juries. *The New York Times* (1871) called abortion "the evil of the age" and estimated that there were 200 practicing abortionists in New York City, not including physicians who sometimes terminated unwanted pregnancies. Most women considered abortion before quickening their right; the notion of sin did not arise until well after the 1869 Papal pronouncement. Illegal abortions were usually "discovered" only if they ended in disaster. Such was the demand that not even occasional convictions suppressed the practice.

Newspapers published numerous advertisements for abortifacients, often referred to as "Portuguese Female Pills." Emmenagogues to stimulate late or irregular menstruation were advertised as "Female Regulators" without mentioning the euphemisms for abortion.

After the founding of the American Medical Association in 1847, organized drives were gradually launched to professionalize medical training and health services, and to obtain legal and public acknowledgement of the professional status of physicians. An antiabortion campaign, portraying physicians fighting the health risks associated with botched abortions and opposing the brazen advertisements of greedy abortionists, seemed a "perfect" way to further these objectives. For example, in 1864, the American Medical Association offered a prize for the most popular antiabortion tract and allied itself with others in a public policy crusade against abortion (*Mohr*, 1978).

After the end of the Civil War in 1865, the antiabortion drive was strongly supported by upper-class, white, Anglo-Saxon Protestants, anxious about declining birthrates among native-born married women and concerned about the reproductive potential of new immigrants. They were eventually joined by antiobscenity crusaders and by feminists, who counseled abstinence as the only sure protection against unwanted pregnancy and perceived abortion as an undesirable byproduct of the suppression of women (*Gordon*, 1976; *Mohr*, 1978).

Between 1860 and 1880, more and more American states dropped traditional quickening doctrines, revoked common-law immunities for pregnant women, and recognized the American Medical Association as the primary arbiter of medical training and practice. The doctrine that interruption of pregnancy at any point was a crime was accepted and remained in force with little change for nearly a century. By 1900, abortion was illegal in all American jurisdictions. In most states, a threat to the life of the pregnant woman was the sole legal ground on which abortion could be performed; in a few, a threat to the woman's health sufficed. Women deciding to terminate unwanted pregnancies for social or economic reasons were forced to seek more dangerous illegal abortions.

Medical Fashions

While the fashions of medical practice varied from country to country after abrogations of common-law liberties, "the position, broadly speaking, was that mainstream medicine increased its disdain for contraception, abhorred abortion, and avoided all issues relevant to human sexuality when it could but, when pressured, recommended abstinence and prayer" (*Davis*, 1974). The lack of modern scientific knowledge, the mood of the medical/legal establishment, and the fear of criminal sanctions combined to limit professional interest in improving the technology of contraception and abortion. A distinguished exception was *James Young Simpson*, the 19th century pioneer gynecologist who introduced anesthesia to midwifery and lectured students on the use of an exhausting syringe attached to a small

14

diameter cannula inserted into the uterine cavity to induce menstruation (*Simpson,* 1872).

From *Simpson's* death until well after the turn of the century, little mention appears in the medical literature on the use of vacuum or tubing. By the early 20th century, medicine rediscovered use of the uterine curette: "sensible small instruments were again available, closely resembling those of the ancient Greeks and Romans, particularly those found at Pompeii and Herculaneum" (*Davis,* 1974).

Initial Liberalization

Differences in historical, cultural, and ideological development have produced considerable variation in legislation on the termination of unwanted pregnancy. In 1920, the Soviet Union became the first country to legalize in-hospital abortion on request of the woman in the first trimester of pregnancy. The liberalization was intended to be temporary, designed to recognize the equal status of women and protect their health. It was believed that as Soviet social conditions improved and the state assumed the burdens of childrearing, abortions would become less necessary and the problem of unwanted pregnancies would cease to exist (*David,* 1970). In 1936, after considerable discussion, legislation was enacted again making abortion a criminal offense except for compelling medical and eugenic reasons. The accompanying commentary justified the 1920 Decree as a "regrettable necessity" (*Field,* 1956). The effect was a dramatic but short-lived increase in the birthrate, which by 1940 had fallen below the 1936 figure.

A modified abortion law was passed in Iceland in 1935, introducing the concept of medicosocial indications (WHO, 1971). Legal history was made in 1938 in London when Aleck Bourne, a gynecologist at St. Mary's Hospital, was acquitted at a trial under the 1861 Offences Against the Person Act. Mr. Justice MacNaughton in *Rex v. Bourne* established the precedent that a physician may perform an abortion if he believes that continuation of the pregnancy would endanger the woman's life or make her "a physical and mental wreck" (*Dickens,* 1966; *Potts,* 1971). The late 1930s also saw modifications of the Danish and Swedish abortion statutes, introducing the concept of socioeconomic indications (WHO, 1971).

Abortion legislation in Germany can be traced from the Prussian Penal Code of 1851 through the 1871 German Reich Penal Code which decreed in Section 218 that a woman found guilty of abortion was liable to up to five years imprisonment. The operator was liable up to life imprisonment, with various extra terms in case of maternal death, but some alleviation if there were extenuating circumstances. Legislation approved in 1926 during the Weimar Republic reduced sentences for the woman to from one day to five years and for the operator from one to 15 years, depending on circumstances. After Hitler came to power, existing legislation was more stringently enforced, except for abortion on eugenic grounds. In 1936, prosecutions doubled from earlier years and harsher sentences were imposed. In 1938,

15

a Jewish couple was acquitted of attempting to procure an abortion on the grounds that Section 218 could not be used for the protection of Jewish embryos (*Potts, Diggory,* and *Peel,* 1977). After the start of World War II in 1939, abortion was strictly prohibited, with the death penalty introduced in 1943 (*Harmsen,* 1950, *Stephenson,* 1975).

The Post-World War II Period

In 1948, Japan adopted its Eugenic Protection Act, making abortion widely available for a broad range of indications, in part to reduce the steeply rising incidence of illegal abortion (*Muramatsu,* 1974). On 25 November 1955, two years after the death of Stalin, the Supreme Soviet repealed the 1936 restrictions in the Soviet Union. The reasons presented were to reduce "the harm caused to the health of women by abortions performed outside of hospitals," and "to give women the possibility of deciding for themselves the question of motherhood" (*Field,* 1956). All of the socialist countries of Central and Eastern Europe except Albania eventually passed similar legislation (*David,* 1970). Changes in abortion legislation in Czechoslovakia are discussed in Chapters 6 and 9.

The People's Republic of China adopted a policy of elective abortion in 1957 (*Chen,* 1970). In 1965, Tunisia became the first Moslem nation to permit abortion on request, initially only for women with five living children; a decade later, this right was extended to all women in the first trimester of pregnancy (*Nazer,* 1972). In the same year, Cuba became the first country in the Caribbean and Latin America to make abortion available without cost and on request of the pregnant woman (*David, 1983*)

The United Kingdom implemented a wide-ranging Abortion Act in 1968, following considerable public and parliamentary discussion (*Simms* and *Hindell,* 1971). The Act does not apply to Northern Ireland, where termination of pregnancy continues to be governed by the 1861 Offences Against the Person Act and the 1945 Criminal Justice Act of Northern Ireland. India passed liberal abortion legislation in 1971, including contraceptive failure as an acceptable indication. In 1972, Zambia became the first African nation south of the Sahara to liberalize abortion, eventually followed by Zimbabwe in 1978.

The German Democratic Republic authorized an abortion on request statute in 1972, promulgating one of the most liberal guidelines then in existence. In January 1973, the U.S. Supreme Court (1973) ruled that during the first three months of pregnancy the abortion decision rests solely with the pregnant woman and her physician. In June of 1973, Denmark became the first European nation, other than the socialist countries of Central and Eastern Europe, to approve legislation permitting abortion as a woman's right during the first trimester of pregnancy. One year later, Sweden recognized the right of the woman, in the absence of medical contraindications, to have her pregnancy terminated up to the 18th week of gestation. A physician may be fined or imprisoned up to six months for refusing to comply with a woman's request for a first trimester abortion or failing to refer her to the National Board of Health. Also in 1974, Singapore amended its already liberal law to permit abortion on request until the 24th week.

In January 1975, France adopted a statute (reaffirmed in 1979) leaving the decision for the interruption of pregnancy to the woman and her physician up to the 10th week of gestation. During the same month, an elective abortion law came into force in Austria. In May 1976, abortion legislation was liberalized in the Federal Republic of Germany. Later that year, Iran, Liberia, and New Zealand also enacted more liberal statutes. During 1977, the trend toward liberalization continued in Israel and Italy, followed by Luxembourg in 1978. In the 1980s, Greece, Spain, Portugal, and Turkey liberalized abortion availability. Kuwait became the first Arab nation on the Persian Gulf to permit abortion for health and eugenic reasons.

Re-restriction

Alarmed by declining birthrates and soaring abortion rates, Romanian authorities drastically restricted abortion in October 1966, limiting availability to women who were over age 45, with four or more living children, or who met explicitly defined physical, mental, or genetic indications (*David*, 1982b). At the same time, importation of contraceptive pills and intrauterine devices was sharply curtailed. In March 1984, Romania reimposed strict enforcement of its abortion statutes, prohibited importation of modern contraceptives, and initiated a policy of monthly pregnancy tests of married women up to age 45. No other country has followed the Romanian example, except Iran, which totally outlawed abortion after the fall of the Shah.

For a time, legal and administrative restrictions were imposed in Bulgaria, Czechoslovakia, and Hungary, but few women in social need were denied termination of an unwanted pregnancy on initial request or on subsequent appeal (*David* and *McIntyre*, 1981). Some re-restrictions, following liberalization, were also imposed in Israel and in New Zealand but have not been strongly enforced. In several other European countries with low birthrates, abortion on request of the pregnant woman, or on broadly interpreted sociomedical or socioeconomic indications, exists side by side with pronatalist population policies.

Current Legal Situation

As of May 1987, the legal status of abortion ranges from complete prohibition (which may or may not be enforced) to elective procedures at the request of the pregnant woman. Population estimates suggest that about 76 percent of the world's 5 billion people live in countries where the dangerous practices of self-induced abortion or pregnancy termination by untrained persons have been replaced by the growing availability of legal abortion performed safely, rapidly, and at relatively low cost on broad health, eugenic, juridical, or social grounds by trained personnel in hospitals or free-standing clinics. Countries whose statutes allow abortion on request account for 39 percent of the world's population. About 24 percent of the population live in nations where abortion is either illegal for any reason or permitted only on narrowly defined grounds to protect the woman's life or health (*Tietze* and *Henshaw*, 1986). However, some abortions on medical grounds are probably tolerated in all countries having restrictive legislation (*Stepan*, 1979).

In retrospect, it is apparent that during the last quarter century a revolution occurred in the realm of abortion legislation. In 1954, abortion was illegal in all countries of the world with the exception of Iceland, Denmark, Sweden, and Japan. In subsequent years, more than 30 countries changed their formerly restrictive laws or policies to permit abortion on request or on a broad range of social indications. The relaxation of abortion laws in diverse countries with different sociocultural heritages can probably be traced to three interrelated reasons: (a) general recognition of the threat of illegal abortion to public health, (b) support for women's rights to terminate an unwanted pregnancy under safe conditions at an early state of gestation, and (c) provision of equal access to abortion for rich and poor women alike. Social and technological changes, coupled with the increasingly vocal demands of well organized women and their male supporters, could no longer be resisted by reluctant legislatures (*Dellapenna*, 1979).

When viewed in historical and sociocultural perspective, fertility regulation, whether by pre- or postconceptive means, is not a new idea. Only the technical possibilities and social attitudes have changed over time. While many individual physicians have consistently championed the rights of women, organized medicine has often been reluctant to support voluntary family planning services unless established under medical control. Such policies have been particularly detrimental to those economically disadvantaged women who wanted to regulate their childbearing but were unable to afford financially costly abortions.

In some respects, the process of obtaining an abortion differs markedly from traditional medical practice. Women wishing to terminate an unwanted pregnancy are usually "healthy" and seldom in need of medical diagnosis or medical treatment of a medically identified disease. Some physicians are prepared to perform abortions to save a woman's physical health, but not to preserve the economic well-being of her family. The role conflict between serving as a technical implementor of a woman's decision and the more traditional orientation and perception of a medical decision maker is at least as great a factor in the abortion debate as the more widely discussed moral issues.

The personal decision to terminate an unwanted pregnancy and the implementation of that decision have all too often in the past depended on prevailing legislation, medical practices, or the opinions of review groups. Only rarely have there been reports on the development of children to whom women gave birth involuntarily. A major problem has been to find such children and follow their development in comparison to matched controls without risking additional difficulties by revealing the study objectives. The varied approaches taken are summarized below and presented in greater detail in subsequent chapters.

The Göteborg Cohort, 1939-42

Planning and conducting a scientific study of the developmental effects of denied abortion requires a legal system that approves certain applications for pregnancy termination and rejects others, along with a national population registration system that facilitates longer term follow-up of women and the children they bore involuntarily. Such conditions existed in Sweden in the late 1950s when Dr. *Hans Forssman*, a psychiatrist, and his social worker colleague, Dr. *Inga Thuwe*, launched their pioneering follow-up study of 120 children born during 1939-42 to Göteborg women whose requests for abortion on psychiatric grounds had been denied by medical authorities. Registered in Göteborg when they were born, they could be followed through the various Swedish population registers for 35 years. For each of the unwanted children, the very next same-sexed child born in the same hospital was selected as a control. As noted in Chapter 4, no effort was made to pair-match the children or to conduct interviews or psychological assessments with them or any other informants.

Nevertheless, the Swedish researchers were able to demonstrate on the basis of available data that individuals born after refusal of an application for a therapeutic abortion are at greater risk than the controls for adverse psychosocial problems during their developmental years with such differences gradually diminishing in adulthood.

Subsequent to the initiation of the *Forssman* and *Thuwe* study, legal abortion in Sweden was liberalized in 1941 and again in 1942 and in 1946. Following these changes in Swedish legislation, important studies were reported by *Höök*, by *Hultin* and *Ottosson*, and by *Blomberg*.

The 1948 Stockholm Cohort

Höök (1963) focused on 249 women whose applications for abortion had been refused by the Swedish National Board of Health in 1948. During free-form interviews initiated in 1955, the women supplied retrospective data about themselves and the children, including their development, health, and adjustment to school life. In addition, *Höök* obtained extensive data on relationships with male partners, subsequent pregnancies, and mental status.

In all, 4,553 applications for abortion were filed in 1948. Of these, 484 (11 %) were refused. To facilitate individual interviews, only the 249 women residing in Stochkolm or in the counties of Stockholm and Uppsala were included in the study.

19

At follow-up, 202 women had 204 living children, who, on average, were 8 $1/2$ years old at time interview.

A total of 172 women (81 % of the delivering women) reared their own children born after abortion had been denied. Only 120 of the 204 living unwanted pregnancy (UP) children (59 %) grew up with both natural parents; 52 of the 172 child-rearing mothers (30 %) were either single parents or married to a man other than the child's natural father.

During the interviews, the women were questioned about their attitude to the pregnancy and to the child. A complex pattern of feelings emerged, with considerable ambivalence expressed. The support provided by the male partner was an important determinant of the woman's perception. The proportion of UP children mentined in the school health records as having experienced a mental disturbance or having been referred to the school psychiatrist was not significantly different from the average of 20 percent noted for all children in the Stockholm school district born in 1948-49. *Höök* (1971a, 1971b) subsequently followed to age 18 the 88 children residing in the Stockholm area. Taking as a paired control the same-sexed classmate with the nearest birthday, she found a preponderance of behavioral and conduct disorders in the unwanted UP boys, many of whom came from more unstable homes and had never known their natural fathers. More UP children (20 %) than controls (12 %) had been registered for delinquency. More details are presented in Chapter 5.

The 1960 Swedish Cohort

By examining the first 2,577 consecutive applications from the beginning of 1960 in the records of the National Board of Health and Welfare, *Hultin* and *Ottosson* (1971) located, 1,008 refusals, representing 39 percent of all applications. They obtained obstetrical records on 783 children born to women denied abortion (UP children). They then collected a control series by taking the woman with the immediately following case record number in the same obstetrical unit of the same hospital who had not requested abortion (AP controls). No significant differences were found regarding fetal development, prematurity, perinatal mortality, or presence of fetal malformations.

Blomberg (1980a) extended the *Hultin* and *Ottosson* series by surveying the remaining refused abortion applications in the 1960 files of the Swedish National Board of Health and Welfare. He found an additional 608 women, of whom 481 had given birth. It was possible to compare each of 480 babies with the immediately next-born baby in the same delivery ward. Combining the *Hultin* and *Ottosson* series with the *Blomberg* series, it was noted that there were many more younger and unmarried women of lower social status among the UP mothers, but no significant differences were found between UP and AP babies in regard to height and weight at birth, when controlled for gestational age and prematurity. However, the incidence of fetal malformation increased with higher age and lower social class among UP women (*Blomberg*, 1980b).

In a related study, *Arfwidsson* and *Ottosson* (1971) reviewed 783 cases from the 1960 abortion register and next-born children, finding no support for the hypothesis that unwantedness as defined in an abortion application might adversely affect pregnancy and delivery. *Blomberg* (1980c) extended this work by matching 131 pairs of UP and AP women for age and parity, as well as reasonable similarity in social status, and arrived at essentially the same conclusion.

Subsequently, *Blomberg* (1980d) examined postnatal, somatic, and psychosocial development over 15 years in 90 pairs of same-sexed UP and AP children born in the same delivery ward whose mothers were of similar age, parity, and social class. School performance of the UP children was significantly worse. Significantly more UP children than AP children were found to have had neurotic or psychosomatic symptoms noted in their school health records. A significantly larger number of UP children (17) than AP controls (5) were registered with the child welfare authorities.

Blomberg observed that all the differences in his study, whether statistically significant of not, were uniformly to the disadvantage of the UP children. When taken together, they led to the conclusion that, in the aggregate, the UP children "grew up in a more insecure environment, performed worse in school, and more often needed treatment for nervous and psychosomatic disorders. There was also a tendency towards worse social adjustment." Further details are presented in Chapter 5.

The Prague Cohort, 1961-63

As shown in Chapters 6 and 7, the Prague study built on the Swedish experience. Unique circumstances combined to provide access to children born during 1961-63 to women twice denied abortion for the same pregnancy, once on original request and again on appeal. Moreover, funds were available to pair-match each of the 110 boys and 110 girls with a control child whose mother had not requested an abortion. The children were matched for age, sex, birth order, number of siblings, and school class. Mothers were pair-matched for age, socioeconomic status (as determined by their and their husbands' educational level), and by the husband's or partner's presence in the home, that is, completeness of the family (there were only very few exceptions in this respect). All the children were reared in two-parent homes, although sometimes with a father substitute instead of the natural father. The matching procedure, which had not been attempted in prior studies, required more than a year to complete. Considerable data became available through extensive questionnaires and interviews conducted with each child, the mothers (and many fathers), and the teachers during three follow-up phases. All the differences noted were consistently in disfavor of the unwanted-pregnancy children. Over the years these differences widened and many that had not been statistically significant at age nine became so at age 16 or 21. While it is difficult to make individual predictions, there seems little doubt that, in the aggregate, unwantedness in early pregnancy has a not negligible effect on later development, influencing quality of life and casting a shadow on the next generation.

The 1966 Northern Finland Cohort

The Northern Finland study follows 12,058 children born in 1966 to women residing in the northernmost provinces who indicated during the 24th or 28th week of gestation whether or not their pregnancies occurred at a propitious time, would have been more desirable later, or should not have occurred at all. At the time, legal abortion was available only on well-defined medical grounds when authorized by two physicians. Most of the women who declared their pregnancies to be unwanted did not meet the strict requirements for pregnancy termination. As noted in Chapter 8, pair-matching control studies, building on the Prague experience, were initiated at age eight and repeated at age 16. On the whole, the Northern Finland studies indicate that unwantedness during pregnancy is frequently associated with less favorable socioeconomic conditions, leading to subsequent developmental problems.

Concluding Note

Subsequent chapters present the rationales that guided the studies of the effects of denied abortion on the subsequent development of children born to women who gave birth involuntarily. The methodology and findings from research in Göteborg, Prague, and Northern Finland are then reviewed in greater detail, followed by an overall discussion of observations, conclusions, and suggestions.

As will be evident from this monograph, and as previously reported by other colleagues, the personal decision to terminate an unwanted pregnancy is usually a private matter. It is affected to only a limited degree by public policies and is typically the end product of complex interaction processes, including psychosocial and socioeconomic determinants, couple communications, and cultural-environmental influences (e.g., *David* and *Friedman*, 1973; *David*, 1974, 1978, 1980). The studies reported here demonstrate, we believe, that involuntary childbearing is rarely conducive to sound public health practice. Unwantedness can pose significant risks for child development, with socially undesirable long-term implications. Hopefully, our attempt to share experiences from Northern and Central Europe will strengthen the worldwide efforts to reduce the incidence of unwanted pregnancy, while maintaining ready access to safe legal abortion for women in need.

Chapter 2

Unwantedness: Demographic and Psychosocial Perspectives

Henry P. David

The general hypothesis that "unwanted" pregnancies can have multiple and damaging effects is hardly new. Nearly 90 years ago, *Freud* (1898) suggested that "it would be one of the greatest triumphs of mankind . . . were it possible to raise the responsible act of procreation to the level of a voluntary and intentional act." The mental health literature reflects the widely shared sentiment, often based on or reinforced by individual case studies, that a child unwanted during pregnancy starts life in an unfavorable position and is likely to receive less parental love, affection, and care than a child wanted at conception (e.g., *Menninger,* 1943; *Caplan,* 1954; *Okpaku,* 1982). Others have written on the circular relationship between unwantedness and poverty, and their relevance for mental health (e.g., *Rainwater,* 1960; *Fleck,* 1964; *Lieberman,* 1964; *Beck,* 1970). Reducing the influence of unwanted motherhood and preventing associated health problems were major motivations for *Margaret Sanger* (e.g., 1916) in her campaign for unfettered access to contraception. Prevention of unwanted pregnancies, especially among adolescents, continues to be a priority concern for the International Planned Parenthood Federation (e.g., 1986), the World Federation for Mental Health (e.g., *David,* 1986b), and the World Health Organization (e.g., *Friedman* and *Edstrom,* 1983).

The negative emotional reactions engendered by an unplanned and unexpected pregnancy have been demonstrated throughout recorded history by the large numbers of women who have resorted to abortion regardless of legal sanctions and often at considerable personal risk (e.g., *David,* 1973a, 1973b, 1981a). In more recent years, following liberalizing legislation and high court decisions in many lands, strongly divergent attitudes have appeared, each attracting dedicated adherents.

There is an implicit assumption among many supporters of the family planning movement that planned pregnancies tend to be intended and wanted at time of conception and that unplanned pregnancies are more likely to be unintended and unwanted. The rationale for this assumption is straightforward: when couples are free to regulate their own fertility and have access to modern methods, they choose what they like and like what they choose (*Miller,* 1983). When events conspire against them, whether through failure in adequate planning or through method failure, and when these failures are compounded by lack of access to safe procedures for terminating an unwanted pregnancy on request in early gestation, couples may react in diverse ways, ranging from complete acceptance of a previously unwanted pregnancy to resorting to illegal abortion.

Quite another view is expressed by those who believe that life begins at conception and that all pregnancies, whether planned or unplanned, should be carried to term because all life, born or unborn, is inherently valuable. Legalization of abortion is opposed, except perhaps when the pregnant woman's life is endangered. Emphasis is less on personal control, self-determination, and choice than it is on a more general perception of preserving life, maintaining established values, and accepting what fate has bestowed. There are, of course, intermediate and conflicting positions, such as occurs when an unforeseen circumstance may change an originally intended pregnancy into an unwanted one, or when legal abortion is tolerated as a lesser evil than an even more unattractive resolution of a problem pregnancy.

Despite numerous case reports, there is little published evidence from carefully controlled studies that the unexpected, unplanned, or unwanted pregnancy has deleterious developmental effects, or that a planned pregnancy more frequently produces a psychologically healthy child. The research literature offers few operational definitions of "unwantedness" and equally few on the relationship of "unwantedness" or "wantedness" to specific objective criteria of physical, mental, or social health or maladjustment. Even less is known about discernible differences between matched samples of "wanted" and "unwanted" children from birth through early childhood, adolescence, and adulthood.

This chapter discusses some of the complexities surrounding the term "unwantedness," noting differences between unintended conceptions, unplanned pregnancies, and children unwanted at birth. Reasons for the inadequacy of current conceptualizations are considered, along with differences in demographic and psychosocial approaches to reproductive behavior. An operational definition of unwantedness is then suggested. Unwantedness is usually associated with other psychosocial factors in complex combinations. Depending on individual circumstances, a family atmosphere is created which has the potential of exerting a significant negative influence on a child's psychosocial development which, in turn, influences longer term emotional satisfactions in relationships with important others in the social environment.

Unintended, Unplanned, and Unwanted

The phenomena of unintended conceptions, unplanned pregnancies, and children unwanted at birth are as old as humanity and probably universal. Still, the concept of unwantedness is vague, elusive, and beset with operational difficulties, whether applied to conception, pregnancy, or birth (e.g., *Pohlman,* 1965, 1969; *David,* 1972). Many actors are involved in any one of these events, are affected by its occurrence or nonoccurrence, and, through actions, pressures, and norms, influ-

24

ence the probability of a specific decision. Thus, despite the considerable significance that reproduction and childbearing have for society, it is not surprising that there is a lack of precision in defining the psychological concepts used to describe and understand the subjective states and overt behaviors associated with decision-making, planning, and adaptive responses related to conception, pregnancy, and birth (e.g., *Miller*, 1978).

It is particularly important, for example, to differentiate between intended and unintended conceptions, between wanted and unwanted pregnancies, and between children wanted or unwanted at birth or afterward (*David* and *Baldwin*, 1979). Motivations regarding wantedness are mutable and often change with fantasies that may be rudely altered by environmental realities. Did the woman want a child but not at time of conception? Was the pregnancy wanted or unwanted by the father? What were the dynamics of the couple interaction, the conditions surrounding conception and pregnancy, and the circumstances of birth and early childhood?

The term "unwanted pregnancy" may have a variety of possible meanings in different psychosocial contexts. A distinction can be drawn between those women whose external socioeconomic circumstances induce them to reject a pregnancy (e.g., poverty, too many other children, being unmarried, etc) and those women whose subjective situation or personal goals (e.g., desire to finish education or to pursue a career) lead them not to want a child, at least at that time (e.g., *Callahan*, 1970). Circumstances under which a pregnancy is deemed tolerable or not differ for different women at different times in their life cycles. A further complicating factor is the interaction between the circumstances of the pregnancy and the values and beliefs of the individuals involved. A small proportion of women might reject (or accept) any pregnancy under any circumstances, while others would require extremely difficult circumstances before rejecting a pregnancy.

In some cultures, the term "wantedness" may be almost meaningless if having children is part of a conventional or traditional institutional pattern. In other societies, there are numerous case histories documenting that some parents who were despondent, or at least ambivalent, about a pregnancy fully accept and love the child after birth. Sometimes parents who said they wanted the pregnancy do not accept the child after birth and show their feelings by abuse or neglect. Means of preventing conceptions or terminating unwanted pregnancies can accomplish little with regard to children who were initially wanted but later became unwanted.

Reasons for Inadequate Concepts

There are at least three reasons for the inadequacy of the concepts used to describe the sometimes subtle psychological states involved in planning and wanting a conception, pregnancy, or child (e.g., *Miller*, 1978). The first lies in the recency of effective control of conception. Although the desire for conception control has been virtually universal in all societies throughout history (e.g., *Himes*, 1936), reliable conception control did not become possible until about the middle of the 20th century. Only after the development of adequate knowledge concerning the physiology and timing of ovulation in humans in the late 1930s (*Dickinson* and *Bryant*, 1938) was it possible to produce such effective chemical and mechanical contraceptive methods as oral pills in the late 1950s and the intrauterine device in the early 1960s.

The second reason for the inadequacy of the concepts involves the biological and psychological complexity of the subject matter. For example, the fetus undergoes radical biological and behavioral changes beginning with conception and continuing through pregnancy. Similarly, the baby — the object of planning and wanting — experiences rapid change from infancy through childhood. Planning for and adapting to the presence of a child is an ongoing long-term process that occurs in conjunction with many other external events and internal changes concurrently affecting the couple, the two primary individuals involved, whose desires and feelings may reinforce or oppose each other.

The third reason for the inadequacy of concepts is because the discipline of demography has long dominated behavioral approaches to studying and understanding reproductive behavior. As one result, the scientific literature is replete with psychological concepts developed by demographers and employed primarily to meet the needs of their theories and empirical methods. Since demographers are more concerned with aggregates of people, their psychological concepts are seldom related to how individuals think and feel. A good example is the frequent confusion in the demographic literature on how to differentiate between psychological antecedents to having a child, such as intending a conception or planning a birth, and the psychological responses to a conception, pregnancy, or birth with feelings such as acceptance or unwantedness.

Incidence of Unwanted Fertility: Demographic Concerns

The first extensive information on unwanted fertility in the United States was provided in the 1955 "Growth of American Families (GAF) Study" (*Freedman, Whelpton,* and *Campbell,* 1959). Fertility was defined as "completely planned" when the couple used contraception regularly and conceived only when they stopped contraceptive practice for the purpose of having a child. "Partially planned fertility" described those couples who did not have more children than they wanted but experienced spacing failures in the sense that some pregnancies occurred considerably earlier (or later) than planned. The concept of "excess fertility" was reserved for those situations when the couple's most recent pregnancy was unwanted then or later by the wife, the husband, or both. The question asked was: "Before your last pregnancy began, did you really want another child at some time in the future, or would you just as soon not have had one?"

Ten years later, in the 1965 National Fertility Study (NFS), the time referent of unwantedness was restricted to the time of conception (e.g., *Bumpass* and *Westoff*, 1970; *Ryder* and *Westoff*, 1971). Assuming reliability of data, it was asserted that such and such number of children would not have been conceived had the couple practiced perfect contraception. However, it was also acknowledged that a couple which had decided not to have additional children could change their mind at a later date. A pregnancy occurring between these points of time would be classified as unwanted but deemed wanted if it occurred subsequent to the change of mind. With this approach, a retrospective as well as prospective conceptualization is required to assess wantedness. In sum, the demographic model of reproduction assumes that children are born mostly on the basis of family size ideals and goals (which may change over time) and that a baby born before the eventually desired goal is reached may represent an unintended conception, that is, a timing or planning failure, but would not be classified as "unwanted."

Reports from national fertility surveys conducted in the United States in the late 1960s and early 1970s (when abortion was illegal) reflect the difficulties demographers encountered when asking retrospective questions (e.g., *Bumpass* and *Westoff*, 1970; *Ryder* and *Westoff*, 1971; *Ryder*, 1973). A similar approach was followed in Cycle III of the National Survey of Family Growth, the latest of seven such surveys of U.S. fertility since 1955 and the first to cover all women of childbearing age. Interviews were held between August 1982 and February 1983 with 7,969 women, representative of 54 million women age 15-44. Again, "wanted births are defined as those that the woman, at the time of conception, wanted to have at some time in her life" (*Pratt et al.*, 1984). These included pregnancies that occurred sooner or later than planned as well as those coming at what was considered the "right time".

The concept of "excess fertility" was changed to unwanted births and restricted to those pregnancies that the mother did not want either at time of conception or at any future time. Considering all the surveys, it has been calculated that unwanted births declined substantially in the United States from around 20 percent in the 1950s and 1960s to 13 percent in 1973 and to 7 percent in 1982 when abortion was legal throughout the country (e.g., *Osborn*, 1963; *Campbell*, 1969; *Ryder* and *Westoff*, 1971; *Westoff*, 1981; *Pratt et al.*, 1984).

The estimate of 20 percent in the 1950s and 1960s may well have been too low since births to women not living with their husbands and out-of-wedlock births to never married women were not represented in the GAF or in the NFS studies. It must also have been difficult for parents to describe as "unwanted" a child who might be nearby during the interview. In addtion, fathers can have a quite different view of the wantedness of the pregnancy, which they may or may not have communicated to their partners, the survey respondents. While present estimates of unwantedness may be low, it is surely correct that a declining proportion of births are described by women as having been unwanted at the time pregnancy was confirmed (e.g., *Munson*, 1977; *Eckard*, 1980; *Rasmussen*, 1983; *Pratt et al.*, 1984).

Psychological Issues

Having criticized demographers, we must also acknowledge that population and reproductive behavior are latecomers to the lexicon of psychology. It is a curious phenomenon that psychologists and other behavioral scientists seriously interested in psychosexual development and the problems of children have given scant attention to the procreative aspects of sex and the possible etiological and epidemiological significance of chance versus planned birth (e.g., *David*, 1971). Indeed, many mental health professionals seem more comfortable discussing sex in the abstract than in confronting the reproductive realities of their patients' lives. For example, the risks of unintended conceptions and unwanted pregnancies facing mentally handicapped persons going on home visits or leave have evoked little interest among service providers (e.g., *David* and *Lindner*, 1975; *David*, 1987).

Although choice is a strong factor in childbearing, chance continues to play a major role in conceiving. While many conceptions result from purposive planning, others can occur by accident even when the couple is trying to prevent conception with a proven contraceptive method. Between these two poles fall conceptions that range from ambivalences about childbearing or about preventing conception and consequent inconsistent efforts to contracept. In the middle are those conceptions which occur as a result of sexual activity unassociated with any intention to conceive or not to conceive (*Miller*, 1983).

Only limited study has been devoted to the decision-making process related to childbearing. There is some evidence that a proportion of couples attempt to rationally evaluate the costs and benefits of childbearing and then try to reach a decision (e.g., *Luker*, 1975; *Burch*, 1980). However, important nonrational elements impinge on the process. Faced with considerable complexity, not only within the reproductive domain but also on the interface with such potentially conflicting domains as sexuality, gender roles, and occupational activities, the human mind, or ego — if you will — is often an inconsistent and inefficient integrator (e.g., *Miller* and *Godwin*, 1977). Other nonrational elements probably derive from the historical recency of human reproductive decision-making and can be related to the considerable importance of social learning in the development of reproductive motivations, attitudes, and beliefs, as well as to the growing ambiguity of social norms in the face of new reproductive technologies and changing reproductive practices (*Miller*, 1983).

Couple decision-making adds a new dimension to reproductive choice because in most instances integration must occur at the level of the individual ego and at the level of the marital dyad or nonmarital partner relationship. Of special consideration are a couple's pattern of communication, its decision role allocation (who decides what), its usual methods of conflict resolution, and the power processes most commonly used by each member. Particularly important are the perceptions the partners have of each other and the accuracy of these perceptions.

Specialists in population and health psychology, concerned with wellness, reducing environmental stress, and improving quality of life, have gradually become attracted to studies of reproductive behavior having practical utility and policy relevance. It was in part for that reason that the World Federation for Mental Health established in 1983 a Committee on Responsible Parenthood which is presently providing technical assistance to pilot projects oriented to reducing unwanted pregnancies among adolescents.

Toward a Definition

It is quite likely that many individuals or couples might disagree with the demographic definitions of wantedness based on timing and planning but not number failures. From a psychosocial perspective, it might be more appropriate to base definitions on behavior, that is, on how a woman coped with her conception. There is no problem in defining a wanted pregnancy as one deriving from an intended conception which the woman wanted to deliver. Unwanted pregnancies and their eventual outcome can be grouped as a continuum, as discussed in the next chapter. The strongest evidence of unwantedness would be reflected in termination of an unintended conception, whether legally or illegally. Next would come those pregnancies for which the woman sought but was denied abortion and eventually delivered and kept the child, as in the Prague and Göteborg studies. A third order of unwantedness would be pregnancies described as unwanted in the late months of gestation, as in the Northern Finland studies. Giving up the baby would be a subcategory.

Thus, for the purposes of this monograph, an "unwanted pregnancy" is defined as a pregnancy that was consciously unintended at time of conception and unwanted during the gestation period. An "unwanted child" is the product of an unwanted pregnancy. The degree of unwantedness may range from resort to illegal abortion, and thus avoiding birth, to delivering the pregnancy after requests for legal abortion have been twice denied for the same pregnancy (as in Prague) or once (as in Göteborg) or when legal abortion is not readily accessible despite an expressed attitude of unwantedness late in gestation (as in Northern Finland).

In this proposed definition of unwantedness, the emphasis is on prospective judgement (intended or unintended conception), not on retrospective aspects or "number failures" (having more children than planned) and not on "timing failures" (having children at the wrong time). It is assumed that the condition of unintendedness and thus unwantedness existed at time of conception and is not the result of a couple later concluding that they made a mistake. Motivation to prevent conception strongly influences effective contraceptive practice, acceptance of legal abortion in cases of contraceptive failure, and the search for and resort to illegal abortion when legal abortion is not available (e.g., *Stampar*, 1973; *Kapor-Stanulovic* and *Friedman*, 1978; *David* and *Rasmussen*, 1980).

Concluding Note

In considering demographic perspectives, it should be recalled that the term "demography" derives from the Greek word "demos," meaning people, and "grafein," meaning to write or to record. However, it is people who decide to be sexually active, people who decide to use or not to use modern contraceptives, and people who decide to foster or neglect family well-being. Although psychology deals with human behavior and populations consist of people, there has been little interface between demography, the scientific discipline that studies human populations in the aggregate, and psychology, the scientific discipline that studies people behaviorally as individuals, couples, or families. There is a strong need for closer interdisciplinary collaboration, to ask not only "how many," but also "why." Within such a context theoretical distinctions may gradually fade as complementary interdisciplinary approaches converge.

Mental health aspects of the developmental effects of wantedness and unwantedness have long been debated with evidence usually selected from individual case reports that do not constitute representative samples. Unintended, unplanned, and unwanted need to be considered in demographic and psychosocial perspective with the aim of evolving an acceptable definition. In addition, it is useful to review diverse gradations on the continuum from extreme unwantedness to extreme wantedness. That is the topic of the next chapter which also considers some views on responsible parenthood and specific areas to be explored in research on this sensitive topic.

Chapter 3

The Wantedness-Unwantedness Continuum and Responsible Parenthood

Zdeněk Dytrych, Vratislav Schüller, and Zdeněk Matějček

In reviewing the concept of unwantedness it is of particular importance to analyze the decision-making process or "coping patterns" in which women or couples engage when confronting the question of whether of not to give birth to a child (e.g., *Janis* and *Mann,* 1977; *David,* 1980). This chapter will suggest a continuum from extreme wantedness to extreme unwantedness, with examples drawn from experience in Prague, to indicate relationships to concepts of responsible parenthood, and to pose some questions for future consideration.

Wantedness — Unwantedness

1. The most extreme form of unwantedness is exemplified by infanticide. Among the children born to Prague women twice denied abortion for the same pregnancy are four whose fate has remained a mystery. While the hospital records confirm their delivery, the mothers adamantly deny their birth and no trace of these four children has ever been found. There is no hard evidence, however, that the babies were actually killed.

2. Another evidence of severe unwantedness is keeping the child in permanent isolation. No one is aware of the child's existence and the mother limits her relationship to the minimum necessary feeding. This leads to symptoms of severe psychological deprivation, also known as Kasper Hauser syndrome. No such cases were noted among the Prague children.

3. A less severe form of unwantedness is apparent in the predelivery decision to give the child up for adoption. This usually involves signing a waiver transferring all rights to the unborn baby to unnamed adoptive parents. There were 16 instances in Prague in which the mother who delivered involuntarily never saw the child after the birth and was not informed of its gender.

4. In another three cases of unwantedness in Prague, the mother cared for the child for a brief period immediately after the involuntary birth and then entrusted it to the care of an institution from which it was eventually adopted. According to then prevailing legislation, a child could be placed for adoption from an institution

31

if the natural parents did not show "sufficient parental interest" for a period of at least one year. (More recently this time limit was reduced to six months.)

5. Unwantedness after involuntary delivery was also shown by those mothers who, soon after birth, permanently entrusted the care of their child to relatives or other persons. Although technically still the mother in a legal sense, the woman maintains only minimal communication with her child. Among the unwanted Prague children, three were living with relatives on a practically permanent basis. It is conceivable that one or more of the four children whose existence was denied by their mothers could also be living under such an arrangement.

6. Among the Prague women twice denied abortion for the same pregnancy, 62 managed not to give birth. No records were located in the appropriate obstetric-gynecological facilities. The probability is very high that they sought and obtained an illegal abortion for their advanced pregnancy, then in its fourth month or later stage. Since their pregnancy records were on file with the abortion commissions, these women accepted a double risk — potential physical harm induced by a late criminal abortion and legal punishment if their action was discovered. This group probably also includes most of the 80 women whose records showed "spontaneous" abortions after their requests for abortion had been denied. A subgroup would consist of those women who decided not to appeal the district commission's rejection of their initial request and obtained an illegal abortion when less than three months pregnant. No cases were found of criminal prosecution for illegal abortion.

7. It is quite likely that some women prefer an illegal termination to an appearance before an abortion commission. They may fear consequences to their reputation, particularly if the unwanted pregnancies are out-of-wedlock or extramarital. The design of the Prague study did not include women seeking abortions outside legal channels.

8. Also excluded from the Prague sample were women whose initial request for abortion was approved, or whose initial request was denied but approved on subsequent appeal, and the scheduled terminations were performed.

9. The women who twice applied for termination of the same pregnancy, were twice rejected, and then delivered the child and kept it became the mothers of the 110 boys and 110 girls who constitute the Unwanted Pregnancy sample of the Prague Cohort. Their children were unwanted in terms of the operational definition described in the preceding chapter.

10. Another group, not included in the Prague study, consists of those women whose requests were initially denied and subsequently approved on appeal, but then did not appear for the scheduled pregnancy termination. Some women appealed the rejection of their initial request but withdrew their appeal or did not appear at their scheduled hearing. For example, of 553 women who appealed to the Prague Appellate Commission during 1961-63, ten (1.8 %) did not attend the proceedings and thus effectively withdrew their appeal. It can only be assumed that they experienced considerable ambivalence about their pregnancy but eventually resolved their conflict by acceptance.

11. Women who did not appeal the rejection of their initial abortion request, accepted the pregnancy, and delivered the child were also excluded from the Prague study. It is assumed that these women experienced somewhat less ambivalence than those who appealed the initial rejection but did not follow through with their appeal.

12. Another degree of ambivalence is experienced by those women who, on discovering their pregnancy, decide they do not want it, attempt termination by primitive means (e.g., hot baths, vigorous jumping up and down, etc.) or consult their general practitioner about possible abortion, but then do not make a formal request, accept the pregnancy, and deliver the child.

13. About nine percent of the control group of Prague mothers of accepted pregnancy children fall into the category of women who neither planned nor wanted the pregnancy but did nothing to terminate it.

14. The majority (56 %) of women in the Prague control group consists of mothers who did not plan their pregnancy but adapted to it and the subsequent birth of the child.

15. Another 34 percent of the Prague control group mothers planned the pregnancy and sought the birth of the child.

16. An even greater degree of wantedness is expressed by those women who longed to have a child after experiencing infertility or extensive social barriers to conception. Their pregnancy is "prayed for," a factor mentioned by just over one percent in the Prague control group.

17. An indication of extreme wantedness would be represented by those women who, for biological or other reasons, are unable to conceive and seek to adopt a child or give birth through one of the newer reproductive technologies. This category is not represented in the Prague study.

The 17 categories described represent only observable behavior and are not meant to be exhaustive. As noted in the preceding chapter, there are numerous other important nuances. An originally planned pregnancy can produce a child unwanted after birth, complicated unconscious drives can trigger negative parental reactions, or compensatory mechanisms may negate original unwantedness.

Responsible Parenthood

The basic premise of responsible parenthood is that every child be a wanted child, reared in an environment providing optimal opportunities for healthy growth and development, both physical and mental. As will be noted in the Prague studies, not every child unwanted during pregnancy remained unwanted. Some became wanted gradually, usually as the result of a variety of interacting factors and circumstances. Thus, a child originally unwanted for seemingly economic reasons may benefit from changing parental attitudes as the economic situation improves. However, no matter how important, economic factors may not be decisive. Parental ma-

33

turity, community support, and the help of friends and grandparents may be equally important contributors to changing the perception of what was once considered a hopeless situation. Experiencing life with a child may also create conditions for changing attitudes from negative to positive.

The small-family norm, initially advocated in Europe and subsequently in North America and Japan, evolved slowly, beginning in the industrialized countries around the start of the 19th century (*Ariès*, 1969). Parents gradually recognized their responsibility to provide material means and education for all their children, not only for the first-born son. As emotional ties between parents and children strengthened, and the costs of rearing children increased, limiting the number of births became an increasingly accepted practice among the more educated segments of society.

In present circumstances, the "one too many" child may not be an actual threat to the economic well-being of the family. It may loom larger as a perceived threat to future plans and the satisfactions of basic psychological needs (e.g., *Fawcett*, 1983; *Oppitz*, 1984). In this sense the distinction between children born unwanted or involuntarily is particularly meaningful and significant.

Future Considerations

For a better perspective on wantedness and unwantedness within the context reported in this monograph, it is necessary to discuss the present situation of the family as perceived in Europe and especially in Czechoslovakia.

Compared with earlier periods in history and unlike the situation in developing countries, the contemporary post-World War II European family is economically far more secure. It is hardly threatened by hunger or major material deprivation. While the arrival of a child may affect the family's standard of living, most of the "threat" is to cultural, cognitive, and other self-actualizing needs. When the child's needs and demands conflict with those of the parents, the question arises about what position the child occupies in the system of family values, and how children accepted positively at the time of pregnancy differ from the children whose births were not wanted.

While some family functions have been replaced by social institutions, the family remains a central factor in the decisive period of childhood, the formation of personality, and integration with society. Unless a family satisfies its members' emotional needs, it crumbles internally and, usually, also externally. How does a family function when forced to accept a child born involuntarily? Does it provide for such a child in the same way it would for a wanted child? Is society threatened by children born from unwanted pregnancies? Does it have to pay a price for insisting that some children be born involuntarily?

In present-day marriage and family formation, highest priority is generally accorded to the strength of the emotional relationship between a man and a woman

34

rather than to any other rational consideration that might have been given priority in earlier days. With the development of the romantic ideal, marriage has also become more fragile, as reflected in the rise of the divorce rate. There is growing recognition that the emotional bond between the marital partners determines the emotional atmosphere of family life, a key component for the child's mental and emotional development, for learning how to give and take emotional stimuli, and for sharing love and affection. Such childhood educational experiences will have a lasting impact on the capacity to experience and fulfill the role of a sexual partner, husband or wife, and parent. Within this context, failure to fulfill the emotional needs of the child and other family members becomes more apparent, with children born from unwanted pregnancies being perhaps most at risk.

Unlike families in earlier times, today's family is quite small in most European countries. Emphasis is on the nuclear family, that is, on parents and children. Ties with the wider family circle are not as close as before, economic interdependence between generations has greatly declined, and the traditional submission in family affairs to decision-making by elders has almost disappeared. Nevertheless, certain values, ideals, and attitudes toward all manner of everyday occurrences still pass from one generation to the next.

It is thus important to ask how and to what extent family background contributes to the formation of a positive or negative attitude of young parents toward their children. What role does it play in rejecting a pregnancy or in the transition toward a more positive view of a child over time?

In a small family, increased demands for better quality upbringing and education are placed on each child. While this is most conspicuous with only children, even two or three children are often exposed to greater parental aspirations than are children in families with five or even more siblings. Parenthood has become less extensive and more intensive, subject to far more parental control amidst protection against external dangers. In this connection, too, it is important to know more about demands made on and performance of children initially rejected during pregnancy.

Another important factor in developing people's attitudes and views of parenthood is the influence of the mass media. In Czechoslovakia, there has been a noticeable shift in the portrayal of the ideal woman, from emancipation in the sense of equal participation in work and social affairs, to the ideal woman-mother who, in addition to her role in work and social activities, achieves undiminished fulfillment in her specific feminine functions of sexual partner, wife, mother, and educator of her children. The question arises about the coping abilities of those women who reject their pregnancy, but are compelled by law to give birth involuntarily.

The women's movement has come a long way in replacing the traditional hierarchical family system with a more democratic one. In Northern Europe, as well as in Czechoslovakia, women have obtained the right to decide the outcome of their pregnancies (during the early stages of gestation) and modern contraceptives are widely available and readily accesible. What does it mean to have been born unwanted and living at this time in such a society? What are the implications for the education of the next generation and for future population policy? These questions will be more specifically considered as the emphasis shifts from unwanted pregnancies and unwanted children to insuring the healthy development of a new generation.

Chapter 4

The Göteborg Cohort, 1939-77

A 35-year Follow-Up of 120 Persons Born in Sweden After
Refusal of Application for Therapeutic Abortion

Hans Forssman and Inga Thuwe

Editors' Note

The Swedish psychiatrist Dr. *Hans Forssman* and his social worker associate Dr. *Inga Thuwe* conducted the first longitudinal study of children born to women denied abortion.These children, born in the years 1939-42 in Göteborg, were followed for 35 years. Begun in the late 1950s, this pioneering Swedish study stimulated subsequent methodologically advanced efforts in Prague and Northern Finland. Drs. *Forssman* and *Thuwe* graciously granted permission to combine their two reports, previously published in *Acta Psychiatrica Scandinavica*, 1966, 42, 71-88 and 1981, 64, 142-149. While we assume responsibility for any errors in restructuring their material for this chapter, authorship properly belongs to our esteemed colleagues *Forssman* and *Thuwe*.

Legal Status of Abortion in 1939

Therapeutic abortion, legally approved in Sweden in 1939, permitted termination of pregnancy (a) when, because of disease, physical defect, or "weakness" in the woman, the birth of the child would endanger her life or health; or (b) when the pregnancy resulted from a felony, such as rape or incest, of from intercourse with a minor girl under age 15, or from intercourse against the woman's will with a man on whom she was economically dependent or who had grossly violated her freedom of action; and (c) when the expected child might inherit a mental illness, mental retardation, or severe physical disorder or deformity from either mother or father. These were the legal grounds for abortion prevailing when the study was initiated. While further liberalization occurred in subsequent years, this study focuses on 120 children born after their mothers' applications for therapeutic abortion on psychiatric grounds had been refused and 120 same-sex control children whose mothers had not requested therapeutic abortion.

The Unwanted Pregnancy Sample (UP)

All the subjects came from Göteborg, Sweden's second largest city, with a population of about 280,000 during 1939-42. The sample includes all women who applied for therapeutic abortion to the Psychiatric Department of Sahlgren Hospital, the city's only large general hospital, during the years 1939-41, inclusive. In all, 197 Göteborg women had 199 applications for legal abortion refused; two women were refused for two separate pregnancies. In 188 instances, the psychiatrist decided against abortion; in ten cases the Medical Board to whom the application had been referred refused authorization for abortion; and in one case, which the Medical Board had approved, the obstetrician refused to perform the procedure because he considered the pregnancy too far advanced.

When the study was launched in the late 1950s, three of the 197 women could not be traced. One had lived in Göteborg for only a short time; the other two may have given false names or temporary addresses. This left 194 women and 196 refused applications. Of these, 68 (or 34.7 %) ended in spontaneous or provoked abortions, many of which were illegal. The women concerned were determined not to carry to term.

The 128 pregnancies (representing 126 women) which could be traced and had not been terminated resulted in 134 children, including six pairs of twins. Of the 134 children, four were stillborn, eight died within one year, one before age two, and one before age three. Of the six sets of twins, two had lost their partners. There remained 120 children, 66 boys and 54 girls, born in the years 1939-42, who could be tracked up to age 21.

The Accepted Pregnancy Control Sample (AP)

All but one of the 120 UP children were registered in Göteborg when they were born. For each of the 102 infants born in a local maternity hospital, the next same-sexed child born in that hospital was selected as a control. For the 17 born elsewhere, the first same-sexed child registered in the city hospitals that same day was chosen as a control. When the control subject died before age 21, it was replaced with the first same-sexed child born after it in the same hospital. Controls for the twins were the next pair of twins, same-sexed or bi-sexed as needed, born in the same hospital. For the twins who had lost their partners, control subjects were selected as if these twins had been singletons. For the one child born outside Göteborg, the control was the next same-sex child registered in the book of the same parish. While no attempt was made to match the children on any other variables, there is reasonable certainty that the mothers had not requested abortion, that is, accepted their pregnancies and carried to term.

Differences between UP Children and AP Controls

The age of the two series of subjects correspond almost to the day. The greatest difference was 25 days fot the twin cases. The mothers of the UP children (unwanted pregnancies) were 30 years old on average at the time they gave birth; the mothers of the AP children (accepted pregnancies) were 28 years old on average. The difference is statistically significant ($.01 > p < .005$).

Norms from the Swedish electoral statistic for the years 1937-40 were used to compare the two samples by social group, based on the father's occupation at the time of birth, or the mother's if she was unmarried. Adopted children (neither of whose adoptive parents were their natural parent) were grouped according to the adoptive father's occupation. However, children adopted by men who became their mother's husbands after they had been born were grouped according to their mothers' occupation at the time of birth. A significantly larger number of UP children were in the lowest social strata (group III) and fewer in groups I and II. However, for 77 subjects in each series the social group was the same. Additional information on social grouping is shown in the tables.

Among the UP children, 32 (26.7 %) were born out-of-wedlock, compared to only nine (7.5 %) of the AP controls. This difference is highly significant ($p < .001$). Among the pairs of children, 86 were matched for mother's marital status; 34 were not. The parents legitimized five of the 32 UP children born out-of-wedlock by marrying two to 24 months after their births, and five of the nine out-of-wedlock AP children did the same two to 33 months later. An additional seven UP children born out-of-wedlock were adopted by others, as was another UP child born in wedlock. None of the AP children were adopted. Sixty of the UP children (50 %) lived with both their natural parents until age 15, compared to 98 of the AP controls (82 %).

Local records showed that 77 (64 %) of the UP children resided in Göteborg until age 21, compared to 85 (70.8 %) of the AP controls. Of the UP children, 21 (17.5 %) had lived in three or more local authority districts, compared to 19 (15.8 %) of the AP controls. Thus, the two series were reasonably well matched for permanency of residence in Göteborg and for the tendency to move from one district to another. There were 55 pairs who had lived their whole 21 years in Göteborg.

Data Sources

Civil and ecclesiastical parish registry offices provided information on whether or not the pregnant woman had delivered a child after her request for abortion had been refused; the addresses of UP and AP children from birth to age 21; and the marital status of the children and whether they had had children themselves. The child welfare boards in the various districts in which the subjects had lived indicated whether any of these names were in their files and, if so, for what reasons. Inquiries were made at child guidance clinics and youth psychiatric centers in the districts of residence, as well as at mental hospitals, psychiatric departments of general hospitals, and psychiatric outpatient services in the districts where the subjects had lived after the age of 15 years. Letters were addressed to all rural and urban psychiatric departments. Since it was impossible to consult with all private practitioners, information received from this source was disregarded.

With the permission of the government, it was possible to scan the Central Penal Register, where every action restricting a person's liberty is recorded, along with impositions of fines and suspension of sentences from juvenile ages to age 21. Inquiries were addressed to social agencies and alcohol treatment centers in those districts where subjects lived after reaching 16, the age at which persons are registered in their own names. Data were obtained from the relevant school districts on educational performance, promotions, and examinations passed prior to university. Additional information was gathered from the annual list of students enrolled at Swedisch universities. Findings indicated there was no need to inquire at facilities for the mentally retarded.

Military service in Sweden is obligatory for men, but not for women. The Swedisch Institute of Military Psychology was asked to provide information about the fitness group into which the male subjects had been classified, whether military service had been completed, and how successfully. Throughout the search for data, care was taken to preserve the confidentiality and privacy of the subjects.

Family and Social Environment

Circumstances pointing to an insecure childhood are noted in Table 4.1. The findings suggest that 72 (60 %) of the UP children had an insecure childhood, compared to 34 (28.3 %) of the AP controls. If the placements in children's homes are disregarded (many were for only a brief stay), the figures change to 65 (54.2 %) UP

Table 4.1. Comparisons between UP children and AP controls for circumstances suggesting insecurity in childhood; the same child may appear in several categories

Circumstances	UP Children	AP Children
Reports to children's aid bureaus about unsatisfactory conditions at home	17	6
Authorities removed child from home	2	0
Placement in foster home	19	4
Placement in children's home	30	10
Parents divorced before child was 15	23	13
Parent(s) died before child was 15	10	5
Born out-of-wedlock and never legitimized	27	4

40

children and 26 (21.7 %) of AP controls. In both instances, the difference is statistically significant ($p < .001$). Children born after refusal of an application for abortion are at greater risk for insecurity in chidhood than are control children whose mothers did not request abortion.

Comparisons between UP and AP Subjects at Age 21

Major findings from the extensive data search are shown in Table 4.2 for the first 21 years of life. The total number of children for whom information on a specific item could be searched is shown for the UP and AP children, respectively, along with the number of children for whom a specific information item was obtained and the percentage this number represented of the total number of children in the respective series. An indication of level of statistical significance is also shown in the table.

Among the statistically significant differences noted in Table 4.2, 34 of the UP children (28.3 %) came to psychiatric attention during their first 21 years, compared to 18 (15 %) of the AP controls. Registered for delinquency with child welfare boards were 22 (18.3 %) of the UP subjects (19 boys and three girls), compared to ten (8.3 %) of the AP controls (nine boys and one girl). Seventeen of the UP children (14.2 %) received some form of public assistance between the ages of 16 and 21, compared to three (2.5 %) of the AP controls.

Additional significant statistical differences were noted in educational achievement. Just 17 (14.2 %) of the UP children had progressed from primary to some sort of secondary education, compared to 40 (33.3 %) of the AP controls. Even among those 77 pairs of subjects who could be matched for social status, only 10 of 77 UP children (13 %) had attained some form of higher education, compared to 21 (27.3 %) of the 77 AP controls. Among the social group III (lowest) children, five of the 95 UP subjects (5.3 %) had had higher education, compared to 17 of the 84 AP controls (20.2 %). For children in the combined I + II higher social grouping, the findings were 11 of 25 UP children (44 %), compared to 28 of 36 AP controls (77.8 %). Thus, the AP controls exceeded the UP children in academic attainment regardless of differences in proportion of different social groups.

There were no statistically significant differences in the proportions found in the penal register or the records for drunken misconduct, registered in classes for the mentally retarded or other remedial subjects, or exempted from military service. However, in all instances the proportions were higher for the UP children.

Since there was some overlap in findings with the same subjects located in several registers, a comparison was made between the UP subjects and AP controls not identified as coming to the attention of any authorities. As shown in Table 4.2, there were 58 such UP children (48.3 %), compared to 82 AP controls (68.3 %), a significant difference. Similar comparisons yielded significant differences for children coming from social group III, for the 77 pairs with parents from congruent

41

Table 4.2 Important differences between UP children and AP control children during the period 0—21 years of age

Variable Studied	UP Children			AP Control Children			Level of Significance of Difference
	Number of UP Persons	Recorded in Category		Number of AP Persons	Recorded in Category		
		Number	Percent		Number	Percent	
Psychiatric consultation and hospitalization	120	34	28.3	120	18	15.0	*
Registration for delinquency at children's aid bureaus	120	22	18.3	120	10	8.3	*
Registration for crime in Central Penal Register	120	10	8.3	120	3	2.5	—
Registration for drunken misconduct	120	19	15.8	120	13	10.8	**
Public assistance between ages 16 and 21	120	17	14.2	120	3	2.5	**
Subnormal educability or ineducability	120	13	10.8	120	6	5.0	—
Higher education[1]:							
Whole series	120	17	14.2	120	40	33.3	***
Subjects in pairs with parents congruent for social group	77	10	13.0	77	21	27.3	*
Subjects with parents in social group III (low)	95	5	5.3	84	17	20.2	**
Subjects with parents in social groups I+II (higher)	25	11	44.0	36	28	77.8	*
Exemption from military service	66	10	15.2	66	4	6.7	—
Not found in any register							
Whole series	120	58	48.3	120	82	68.3	**
Subjects in pairs with parents congruent for social group	77	34	44.2	77	54	70.1	**
Subjects with parents in social group III	95	40	42.1	84	54	64.3	**
Subjects with parents in social groups I+II	25	19	76.0	36	28	77.8	—
Subjects living the whole period in Göteborg	55	20	36.4	55	38	69.1	***
Subjects living with both natural parents to age 15	60	33	55.0	98	68	69.4	—

[1] More advanced studies than are required by the school law.

* p < .05; ** p < .01; *** p < .001

social groups, and for the subjects living their entire life in Göteborg, but not for subjects in social groups I + II combined or of children who had lived with both their natural parents until age 15.

Conclusions at Age 21

The findings at age 21 showed that UP children were more often reared in unstable and less emotionally secure home situations than the AP controls, who more often lived with their natural parents. The most consistent difference noted, regardless of social grouping, was that UP children achieved a lower level of education than did the AP controls. These observations, plus the differences recorded in the various registers, even when not reaching statistical significance, suggested that children born to mothers refused a legal abortion are born into a worse psychosocial situation than are other children. The very fact that a woman applies for legal abortion, no matter how trivial her grounds may appear to some, means that the prospective child she may be forced to bear runs a risk of having to surmount greater social and mental handicaps than children born to women who do not request abortion.

Follow-Up at Age 35

In the summer of 1977, when all the study participants had completed their 35th year, a further follow-up was conducted. After it had been ascertained where the study and control subjects had resided up to their 35th birthday, it became possible to obtain data from the previously mentioned registers and parish authorities. In the period from age 21 to age 35, one UP male committed suicide; he and his control were followed only up to that event. Four subjects left Sweden for a while, but follow-up was continued when they returned. So many subjects had migrated from Göteborg that the category of life-long residents was dropped.

Findings from the registers are presented in Table 4.3, using the same format as in Table 4.2. The first four items are, of course, linked. Abusers of alcohol are most likely to appear in the penal register, come more frequently to psychiatric attention, etc. For this reason, the last four lines compare the UP subjects and the AP controls whose names did not appear in any of the registers, as was also done in Table 4.2 summarizing findings at age 21. While the UP subjects have more frequent records of social and psychiatric disabilities than the AP controls in the period between 21 and 35 years, the differences are not statistically significant. The only significant difference appears in the comparison of UP subjects and AP controls in social groups I and II who did not appear in any register.

Table 4.4 combines all the observations made over 35 years, including the information on school life and military service previously presented in Table 4.2. All

43

Table 4.3. Registrations during the period 21–35 years of age for UP children and AP controls

Variable Studied	UP Children			AP Control Children			Level of Significance of Difference
	Number of UP Persons	Recorded in Category Number	Percent	Number of AP Persons	Recorded in Category Number	Percent	
Psychiatric consultation and hospitalization	120	29	24.2	120	22	18.3	—
Registration for crime in Central Penal Register	120	14	11.7	120	8	6.7	—
Registration for drunken misconduct	120	16	13.3	120	7	5.8	—
Public assistance	120	20	16.7	120	17	14.2	—
Not found in any register							
Whole series	120	74	61.7	120	89	74.2	—
Subjects in pairs with parents congruent for social group	77	46	59.7	77	55	71.4	—
Subjects with parents in social group III (low)	95	56	58.9	84	58	69.0	—
Subjects with parents in social groups I+II (higher)	25	16	64.0	36	32	88.9	*

p values – see Table 4.2.

Table 4.4. Survey of differences between UP children and AP control during the period 0-35 years of age

Variable Studied	UP Children			AP Control Children			Level of Significance of Difference
	Number of UP Persons	Recorded in Category Number	Percent	Number of AP Persons	Recorded in Category Number	Percent	
Psychiatric consultation and hospitalization	120	52	43.3	120	37	30.8	—
Registration for crime or delinquency	120	28	23.3	120	20	16.7	—
Registration for drunken misconduct	120	25	20.8	120	15	12.5	—
Public assistance during period 16–35 years of age	120	30	25.0	120	19	15.8	—
Subnormal educability or ineducability	120	13	10.8	120	6	5.0	—
Higher education[1]:							
Whole series	120	17	14.2	120	40	33.3	***
Subjects in pairs with parents congruent for social group	77	10	13.0	77	21	27.3	*
Subjects with parents in social group III (low)	95	5	5.3	84	17	20.2	**
Subjects with parents in social groups I+II (higher)	25	11	44.0	36	28	77.8	*
Exemption from military service	66	10	15.2	66	4	6.7	—
Not found in any register							
Whole series	120	42	35.0	120	65	54.2	**
Subjects in pairs with parents congruent for social group	77	27	35.0	77	42	54.5	*
Subjects with parents in social group III	95	29	30.5	84	40	47.6	*
Subjects with parents in social groups I+II	25	14	56.0	36	25	69.4	—

[1] More advanced studies than are required by the school law.
p values – see Table 4.2.

known criminal offenses are listed under one heading; there is no subdivision into records from the child care committees or from the central criminal register. With the extended observation period, the previously noted statistically significant differences have disappeared for psychiatric consultation and hospitalization, registration for crime or delinquency, and public assistance. The differences in educational level reached remain as before; so do differences in not appearing in the registers (which have, however, decreased slightly in statistical significance).

There were no statistically significant differences in marital status or events. Of the UP subjects, 98 married, as compared to 114 among the AP controls. It is not known to what extent the unmarried study participants lived in "marriage-like" cohabitation. There were 25 divorces among the UP subjects (two had two divorces each), compared to 22 divorces among the AP controls (none more than once). Among the UP subjects, 27 were childless, compared to 24 of the AP controls. There were 213 children born to 93 UP subjects and 205 children born to 96 AP controls.

Conclusions at Age 35

Observations over the entire 35 years show a decrease in differences between the UP subjects and AP controls, although the UP subjects continue to show more frequent records of social and psychiatric difficulties than the AP controls. Conversely, more AP controls than UP subjects were never identified in any of the registers. The Göteborg study thus suggests that persons born after refusal of an application for therapeutic abortion are at greater risk for adverse psychosocial problems during their developmental years but that these differences between UP subjects and AP controls diminish in adulthood.

Chapter 5

Additional Studies from Sweden

Henry P. David

Until 1921 all abortions peformed in Sweden were considered illegal and punishable by law. In that year, the Penal Code was amended to allow abortion on "medical grounds" if the woman's life was at risk or if there was a serious danger to her health (*Jonsson, 1976*). To reduce the incidence of illegal abortions and on the recommendations of a National Committee, the law was liberalized in 1938 with therapeutic abortion permitted as of 1 January 1939 for the reasons cited in the preceding chapter.

Swedish abortion legislation was further liberalized in 1941, 1942, and 1946. In the 1940s and early 1950s, several Swedish studies were published on the effects of abortion on women. In the latter part of the 1950s, studies regarding the influence of denied abortion on children born from unwanted pregnancies were initiated by *Forssman* and *Thuwe* (1966) and by *Höök* (1963)

This chapter summarizes the findings reported by *Höök*, who followed children born to women denied abortion in 1948, and by *Arfwidsson, Blomberg, Hultin,* and *Ottosson,* who studied the records of children born to Swedish women denied abortion in 1960. The Swedish Abortion Act was further revised by the law of 1974, giving the woman the right to abortion on request up to the 18th week of pregnancy if there are no medical contraindications. Abortion may also be granted at a later time if the National Board of Health and Welfare concurs that the woman's life or health is seriously endangered. A unique feature of the Swedish law is that a physician may be fined or imprisoned for up to six months for refusing to comply with a woman's request during the first trimester of an unwanted pregnancy.

The 1948 Stockholm Cohort

When *Höök* (1963) began her individual interviews in 1955, she focused on 249 women whose applications for abortion had been refused by the Swedish National Board of Health in 1948. In that year, the proportion of refusals was only 11 percent of all abortions, one of the lowest figures recorded in official Swedish statistics. As will be noted later, a refusal rate of 38 percent prevailed in 1960 when *Hultin* and *Ottosson* (1971) and *Blomberg* (1980a, b, c, d) collected their data from the Swedish National Board of Health.

Höök's monograph (1963) notes the extensive documentation registered with the National Board of Health at the time of application for legal abortion. Included in the material were medical and social reports on the woman's health and life situation, plus records of intelligence tests, comments by relatives, medical examination of the partner, etc.

In the follow-up study, census data and parish records provided information on the place of current residence of the woman, family background, occupation, and marital status, as well as data concerning present and past husbands. Records from midwives and delivery hospitals were reviewed regarding the pregnancy and the delivery of the children born after abortion refusal. During the free-form interview, the women supplied retrospective data about themselves and the children, including their development, health, and adjustment to school life. All interviews exceeded two hours in length. Information obtained was later verified with hospital records, school reports, census registers, and parish files. In addition, *Höök* obtained extensive data on relationships with male partners, subsequent pregnancies, and mental status.

In all, 4,553 applications for abortion were filed in 1948. Of these, 484 (11 %) were refused. To facilitate individual interviews, only the 294 women residing in Stockholm or in the counties of Stockholm and Uppsala were included in the study. It was noted that seven women had left Sweden by 1955; 24 women had appealed their refusal and then obtained the desired permission for abortion from the National Board of Health; and three women had died. Of the remaining 260 women, 249 (96 %) could be persuaded to participate in the personal follow-up, which was conducted over a period of about 4.5 years, starting in the autumn of 1955. The mean interval between application for abortion and follow-up was 9.2 years. At the time of their request for abortion, 48 percent of the women were married, 8 percent widowed or divorced, and 44 percent unmarried. Mean age was 30.0 years for the married, 31.6 years for the widowed and divorced, and 23.2 years for the unmarried. Social class distribution, judged in terms of the male partner's occupation, was similar to that in the general population of Sweden.

Of the 249 women whose request for abortion had been denied, 36 avoided delivery. Of these 22 (9 %) had obtained an abortion through illegal channels, six (2 %) had self-induced abortions, and eight (3 %) experienced spontaneous abortions. Of the spontaneous abortions, two occurred before the woman received notification that her application for abortion had been refused. The remaining 213 women gave birth to 215 children, of whom five died from congenital anomalies or birth injuries during the immediate postnatal period; two others died during the first year, and two more during the second year. These findings are not significantly different from the average for Sweden during the same time period. At follow-up, 202 women had 204 living children who, on average, were 8.5 years old at time of interview.

It was noted that 14 women had given up the child for adoption. When calculated on the number of children born out-of-wedlock, the adoption incidence was 16 percent. An additional 16 children were placed in permanent foster care, two with their natural fathers, seven with their maternal grandparents, and seven in foster homes. A total of 172 women (81 % of the delivering women) reared their own children born after abortion had been denied (UP children). Only 120 of the 204 living UP children (59 %) grew up with both natural parents; 52 of the 172 child-rearing mothers (30 %) were either single parents or married to a man other than the child's natural father. Of the 143 women who had conceived out-of-wedlock, 48 (34 %) had been able to raise the child in a complete home, which was still in existence at time of follow-up.

During the interviews, the women were questioned about their attitude to the pregnancy and to the child. A complex pattern of feelings emerged, with considerable ambivalence expressed. About 73 percent of the women indicated satisfaction with the way their situation had resolved, apparently having eventually adjusted to their life situation, while 27 percent still wished they had not been compelled to deliver their pregnancies. Among those married to the partner either at the time of abortion application or subsequently, 80 percent were satisfied at follow-up, compared to 58 percent of those who had not married the child's father.

The woman's health and adjustment at follow-up were also examined. Of the women who had given birth, 22 percent still showed signs of mental illness and poor adjustment at follow-up. Half of the women (51 %) had shown symptoms of mental disturbance and great emotional strain for a period of considerable length during the period since the birth, but seemed to have overcome their problems. Only 27 percent of the women had been able to cope fully with the pregnancy and the child in question subsequent to the denial of the abortion. The woman's personality was of major importance for her capacity to adjust, as was the support of her partner. Single women diagnosed as having a deviant personality were not adjusted at follow-up in 44 percent of the cases, compared to 35 percent of similar married women. Women with normal personality were not adjusted at follow-up in 17 percent of cases if they were single and in 3 percent if they were married at the time of applying for abortion.

Among the 112 children attending Stockholm schools, 25 (22 %) were mentioned in the school health records as having experienced a mental disturbance or having been referred to the school psychiatrist or to another psychiatrist or to another psychiatric service for observation during their first three or four school years. This proportion was not significantly different from the average of 20 percent noted for all children in the Stockholm school district born in 1948-49.

Höök (1971a, 1971b, 1975) subsequently followed to age 18 the 88 UP children still residing in the city of Stockholm. As a paired control, she took the same-sexed classmate with the nearest birthday. This follow-up was based on an extensive personal interview with each child, including a psychiatric assessment. Each child was also given a projective psychological examination (Holtzman Inkblot Technique and Machover Draw-a-Man test), administered by a trained psychologist. The information thus obtained was complemented by data from the Census register, and by reports from registers reporting social and economic assistance, alcohol problems, and delinquent or criminal behavior. School health records, as well as records from hospitals and child guidance clinics, were scrutinized. *Höök* found a preponderance of behavioral and conduct disorders in the UP boys, many of whom came from more unstable homes and had never known their natural fathers. Similar findings were not noted for the UP girls. There were also significantly more UP than AP boys who showed symptoms of borderline conditions (psychoses) at 18 years of age.

More UP children (20 %) than AP controls (12 %) had been registred for criminality. Compared to the AP controls, the majority of the UP children were rated lower in emotional maturity (relative to chronological age). However, there was no statistically significant difference in overall school performance, as measured by post-junior high school studies, between study participants and other Stockholm students of the same age.

At 23 years of age, the entire Stockholm cohort was again studied, and the results presented to the Swedish National Commission Revising the Abortion Act. For this study, a personal letter was sent together with a questionnaire to all the UP children and the AP controls. Information was also gathered from social registers, from police courts, and from the central criminal register. The files of health insurance offices were studied with regard to sick leave, sick pension, and economic status; whether the person worked or was unemployed, type of work, etc. Reports from the Military Service (males) provided information on general health, intelligence, capacity to serve in the armed forces, etc.

At age 18 significantly more UP children than AP controls had received economic assistance. This difference was more marked at age 23, and related to the mother's level of maladjustment at follow-up. In the group of children whose mothers had adjusted well, no such difference was noted.

The UP children also had a higher incidence of sick leave up to 23 years of age than the AP controls. This difference was more marked in girls, and was similarly related to their mothers having had difficulties in adjustment to the denial of abortion. The frequency of UP children with psychiatric sick leave at the age of 23 did not differ from the AP controls or from the average in Stockholm.

In the questionnaire which was sent to the UP children and the AP controls at 23 years of age (the whole cohort), low self-esteem and signs of depression were reported more often by the girls than by the boys in the UP group.

Criminality was significantly more frequent among the UP boys at 18 years of age, especially if their mothers had had difficulties in adjustment. In the period of 18 to 23 years, criminality was registered only among children whose mothers had had adjustment difficulties.

When the UP children were 35 years old, a check was made with the Census register in order to follow the life events of these subjects, to learn about their adaptability to stress, and, if possible, to study the effect of abortion denial on the third generation. In the period from 16 to 35 years of age, five UP children died (24 per 1,000). The national death rate for men aged 15 to 34 years in the period under consideration varied between 4.56 and 3.88 per 1,000, and for men and women aged 15 to 34 in this period the combined death rate varied between 6.67 and 5.51 per 1,000. This finding suggests that the risk of death for UP subjects is four to six times that of the general population in Sweden. Further findings are expected from this study.

The 1960 Swedish Cohort

Although legal abortions had been available since 1938 and the law was further liberalized in 1941, 1942 and 1946, a more conservative attitude prevailed in 1960 when 38 percent of all applications for abortion were refused by the National Board of Health and Welfare. This was the highest refusal rate recorded in Sweden until then and was never exceeded in subsequent years. By examining the first 2,577 consecutive applications from the beginning of 1960 in the records of the National Board of Health and Walfare, *Hultin* and *Ottosson* (1971) located 1,008 refusals, representing 39 percent of all applications. After writing to the parish registers, they obtained information on 994 women; the remaining 14 were mostly from other countries and could not be traced. Of the 994 pregnant women whose requests for abortion had been denied, 807 (81.2 %) had carried to term, a somewhat higher percentage that the 65 percent noted by *Forssman* and *Thuwe* in 1939-42, when more restrictive legislation led a larger proportion of women to seek illegal terminations of unwanted pregnancies, but lower than the 86 percent observed during the more liberal year of 1948.

Hultin and *Ottosson* received obstetrical records on 783 children born to women denied abortion (UP children). They then collected a control series by taking the woman with the immediately following case record number in the same obstetrical unit of the same hospital who had note requested abortion (AP controls). It was believed that this pairing procedure assured reasonable uniformity of mother's domicile and geographic location, similarity of medical treatment during pregnancy and delivery, and equality in the amount of observation and judgment about complications. Comparisons were based entirely on obstetrical case records without consideration of demographic or social factors. No significant differences were found regarding fetal development, prematurity, perinatal mortality, or presence of fetal malformations.

Blomberg (1980a) extended the *Hultin* and *Ottosson* series by surveying the remaining refused abortion applications in the 1960 files of the Swedish National Board of Health and Welfare. He found an additional 608 women, of whom 481 had given birth. Using the same method of inquiring at parish offices, it was possible to compare each of 480 babies with the immediately next-born baby in the same

50

delivery ward. Combining the *Hultin* and *Ottosson* series with the *Blomberg* series, it was noted that there were many more younger and unmarried women of lower social status among the UP mothers, but no significant differences were found between UP and AP babies in regard to height and weight at birth, when controlled for gestational age and prematurity. However, the incidence of fetal malformation increased with higher age and lower social class among UP women (*Blomberg*, 1980b).

In a related study, *Arfwidsson* and *Ottosson* (1971) reviewed 783 cases from the 1960 abortion register and next-born children, finding no support for the hypothesis that unwantedness as defined by a denied abortion application might adversely affect pregnancy and delivery. *Blomberg* (1980c) extended this work by matching 131 pairs of UP and AP women for age and parity, as well reasonable similarity in social status, noting that only half as many UP as AP women were married at the time of the child's birth. The pair-matched study supported *Arfwidsson's* and *Ottosson's* earlier conclusion that an initially unwanted pregnancy does not predict complications during pregnancy, delivery, or puerperium.

Subsequently, *Blomberg* (1980d) examined postnatal, somatic, and psychosocial development over 15 years in 90 pairs of same-sexed UP and AP children born in the same delivery ward whose mothers were of similar age, parity, and social class. Comparisons were made on the basis of school grades, school health cards, and social welfare registers, following the method used earlier by *Forssman* and *Thuwe* (1966) and described in Chapter 4. A statistically significant number of the UP mothers were unmarried at time of delivery ($p < .001$). Only about half as many UP children as AP controls (39 vs. 68) lived with both natural parents at age 15 ($p < .001$). While there were no significant differences in height and weight of UP and AP children at birth or at ages 7, 11, and 14 years, school performance of the UP children was significantly worse in terms of overall grade averages ($p < .01$), and in Swedish ($p < .01$) and in mathematics ($p < .05$).

Significantly more UP children (30) than AP children (16) were found to have had neurotic or psychosomatic symptoms noted in their school health records; seven UP children, compared to one AP control, had been referred to a psychiatrist. A significantly larger number of UP children (17) than AP controls (5) were registered with the child welfare authorities. For ten UP children, as compared to four AP controls, this registration was for social maladjustment in the form of theft or alcohol abuse. Of the 90 pairs of children, 59 UP children or parents, as compared to 76 AP children or parents, had never been registered with the social welfare authorities ($p < .01$). When the comparison was limited to the 33 pairs of children who lived with both natural parents to age 15, only differences in school grades remained statistically significant ($p < .05$). Other differences, though no longer significant, continued to be in disfavor of the UP children.

Blomberg observed that all the differences in his study, whether statistically significant or not, were uniformly to the disadvantage of the UP children. When taken together, they led to the conclusion that, in the aggregate, the UP children "grew up

51

in a more insecure environment, performed worse in school, and more often needed treatment for nervous and psychosomatic disorders. There was also a tendency toward worse social adjustment." These findings are similar to those previously noted by *Forssman* and *Thuwe* in Göteborg a generation earlier, by *Höök* in the Stockholm cohort of 1948, and subsequently reported from Prague for children born at about the same time.

Chapter 6

The Prague Cohort Through Age Nine

Zdeněk Matějček, Zdeněk Dytrych, and Vratislav Schüller

Background

In December 1957, the Government of Czechoslovakia liberalized its abortion statute, stating that "permission for termination of pregnancy may be granted on medical grounds or for other reasons deserving special consideration" during the first three months of gestation (Czechoslovakia, 1959). As established in practice, the "other reason" were interpreted to include a broad range of economic and social indications. However, applications were not routinely approved. Requests were denied mostly for reasons of health (such as simultaneous occurrence of acute or chronic illnesses that might increase risks likely to be associated with pregnancy interruption), or because the woman was more than 12 weeks pregnant, or because a pregnancy had been terminated during the immediately preceding six months (later extended to 12 months). The decision whether to approve or deny a woman's request for pregnancy termination was the task of the District Abortion Commission, which usually included among its members a gynecologist, a social worker, and a local representative of the trade unions or of the Federation of Women. If the District Abortion Commission denied the woman's request, she had the right to appeal to a Regional Abortion Commission, whose decision was deemed final (*David,* 1970a).

During the first decade of the operation of the 1957 statute, 92 percent of all abortion requests were approved on initial application to the district commissions, with an additional 6 percent approved on appeal to the regional commissions. Only 2 percent of all requests were refused on initial application and again on appeal. The situation then prevailing in Czechoslovakia made it possible to define "unwantedness" operationally in terms of requesting or not requesting termination of a specific pregnancy. Appealing a denial and making a second request to terminate the same pregnancy constituted further empirical confirmation that the pregnancy was "unwanted," at least at that stage of prenatal development.

While the proceedings of the abortion commissions are confidential, fortuitous circumstances made it possible to gain access to the 1961-63 records of the Prague Appellate Abortion Commission for a double blind study carefully safeguarding the identity of all subjects. It became feasible to track all those women who twice requested and were twice denied abortion for the same pregnancy in Prague during 1961-63 (*Schüller* and *Stupková*, 1966, 1972; *Matějček* et al., 1970). The children born to these women and living in Prague constitute the Unwanted Pregnancy (UP) group of the Prague Cohort.

Subsequent sections of this chapter describe factors facilitating the study, the sample selection procedure, and the process of obtaining pair-matched controls. Hypotheses are discussed, methods of data collection and analyses presented, and findings reported from the first follow-up study when the children were about nine years old. Additional follow-up studies, conducted at ages 16-18 and at ages 21-23, are described in the next chapter. Confidentiality has been and still is being preserved. Only one person, the colleague responsible for the matching process, knows which subject belongs to which subgroup. The research project is known in Czechoslovakia as a longitudinal study of Prague children. Participation was rewarded by a token gift. The topic of wantedness or unwantedness of the particular pregnancy which resulted in the birth of a study subject was approached only once, as the final question of the psychiatric interview with the mother during the first follow-up.

The scaled question was phrased as follows:
1. The child was definitely wanted and planned (contraception was discontinued or never practiced);
2. The child was wanted and, although not exactly planned, was expected;
3. The child was not planned and not expected, but, once on the way, was immediately accepted;
4. The child was unwanted and the pregnancy was hard to accept but termination was never considered; and
5. The child was definitely unwanted, the pregnancy was a source of unhappiness, and abortion was considered or requested.

Facilitating Factors

The Czechoslovak system of health care uses a unified set of data records, including records of the mother's visits to the prenatal dispensary, the delivery history, the obligatory pediatric examinations during the child's first years of life, visits to pediatric outpatient clinics, etc. As a child moves, his or her health records are forwarded to the pediatric clinic serving the area in which the new domicile is located. An adult file is initiated when an individual reaches age 18. These records are obtainable for research purposes and make it possible to reconstruct, to a certain extent, the physical and mental health development of any child, adolescent, or adult. The uniformity of the Czechoslovak educational system from elementary schools through universities, and reliance on a standard curriculum and teaching methods, further facilitate the gathering and analyzing of independent data related to study participants.

Essential to the study and its continuation over nearly two decades was the existence of the Central Population Register (CPR), which lists the home address of every adult residing in Czechoslovakia. Without the availability of this unique resource, it would not have been possible to find and verify the addresses of women nine years after they had initially requested an abortion, or to follow study participants into their adolescent and adult years. Moreover, access to the CPR and other local, regional, and national registers provided additional objective data collected entirely independently of the research project.

SAMPLE SELECTION

UP Children

Of the 24,989 applications for abortion in 1961-63, 638 (2 %) were rejected on initial request and on subsequent appeal. As shown in Table 6.1, after excluding 83 women who were not Prague residents or were citizens of another country, there re-

Table 6.1. Terminations of pregnancies and reasons why mother and child could not be examined

Requests for abortion definitely denied	638
Applicants lived outside Prague or were aliens	83
Granted interruption by another commission	43
Women were not pregnant	6
"Spontaneous" abortions	80
Moved from Prague	31
Gave false address	9
Were not found for other reasons	8
No record of the termination of pregnancy	62
Gave birth to a child and lived in Prague	316
Child died in infancy or later	6
Child adopted	19
Parents moved from Prague or left the country	39
Child permanently in institutional care	2
Mother refused to cooperate	7
Child could not be examined for other reasons	6
Mother stated that she did not now or ever have a child although according to reliable evidence she gave birth to one	4
Suitable control child not found	13
Final number of matched and investigated children	220

mained 555 women whose request for termination of an unwanted pregnancy had been twice denied. By 1971, it had been confirmed that 316 (57 %) of the 555 women carried their pregnancies to term while resident in Prague. Of the remaining 239 women, 43 had obtained legal abortions after requesting termination from another district abortion commission either in or outside the City of Prague; 80 were alleged to have aborted spontaneously (a percentage twice that normally expected); six were found not to have been pregnant; 31 had moved out of the city before giving birth; 62 had no record of having given birth at any of the Prague clinics for obstetrics and gynecology and may have resorted to illegal termination; nine gave false addresses on their abortion applications and could not be followed; and eight were untraceable for other reasons.

The 316 traceable Prague women who had carried their pregnancies to term gave birth to 317 live children; of these, six died (five during the first year and one at age eight), a lower proportion of infant mortality than the Prague average during the study period. Nineteen children were adopted, a proportion exceeding the national average by more than 30 times; 16 were offered for adoption before age one and another three children before age three. An additional 39 children moved with their parents from Prague. Two were permanently placed in institutional care; one was severely mentally retarded. Only seven mothers refused to cooperate with the research project; of these, one lived with her husband and six were unmarried or divorced. These families were repeatedly visited by a social worker and by a psychiatrist who reported that their life situations reflected serious psychopathologies. In four cases the mother denied ever having had a child and had none in her care, although reliable evidence existed that she had delivered one. Six women were unable to participate for other reasons; three had died (including the mother of the twins) and the children of three others were living more or less permanently with relatives in rural areas. The remaining 233 women and their children were located in Prague when the research study was initiated in 1971. However, 13 of the children could not be successfully pair-matched, thus reducing the final sample to 220 children, 110 boys and 110 girls. All the children and their mothers were examined (together with the majority of fathers) in the initial round.

It should be noted that the UP sample derives from the 316 women (57 %) who accepted the Appellate Abortion Commission decision, delivered the pregnancy, and raised the child. These women were not as close to the extreme negative end of the wantedness/unwantedness continuum as the 239 women (43 %) of the original 555 women whose motivation to terminate may have been stronger, and who managed to avoid giving birth and are not included in this study. Consequently, the appearance of marked deviations in the psychosocial development of the UP children would, in our view, increase their importance and validity even further.

AP Children

Efforts were initiated to pair-match each UP child with an accepted pregnancy (AP) control child whose parents either purposely stopped some form of contraception in order to have a child, or, if the pregnancy was not deliberately planned, accepted it and did not try to terminate through abortion. Pair-matching of children was for age, sex, birth order, number of siblings, and school class. Mothers were pair-matched for age, socioeconomic status as determined by their and their husbands' educational level, and by the husband's or partner's presence in the home, that is, completeness of family. Almost all of the children were reared in two-parent homes, although sometimes with a father substitute for the natural father.

An extra number of AP control children were selected in case some of their mothers had indeed asked for an abortion. This precaution proved warranted because 7.5 percent of the initial group of AP control mothers stated that they had attempted to terminate their pregnancies by means of legal or illegal abortion. These mothers and their children were excluded from the AP sample and replaced by others from the reserve pool. Since 36 percent of the UP women (that is, those twice requesting an abortion for the same pregnancy) declared their pregnancy to have been welcome or positively accepted from the very beginning (when asked about its wantedness nine years later), it cannot be ruled out completely that a few women remained in the AP sample who once asked for an abortion but denied it later on direct questioning. The number of such AP women is probably negligible and not sufficient to question the results of the study. It does mean, however, that the AP control sample is probably not at the positive extreme of the wantedness/unwantedness continuum. Most likely, the AP group spreads over the whole continuum from children greatly wanted to those forcedly accepted, representing a cross-section of the population. If the UP and the AP groups do not represent either extremes on the continuum, then whatever significant differences are found are likely to be of even greater importance.

The Matching Process

To include as many of the UP children in the study as possible, it was necessary to accept slightly less than perfect matching. The criteria of age and sex were met for all the children. Only children were matched with only children. Birth order matching was also attainable because many of the UP children were first or second born. It was, however, unavoidable to match some of the three-child UP families (where one or two additional children were born after the UP child) with two-child AP families. In all, it was possible to obtain suitable controls for 220 of the 233 UP children. By chance, there were 110 boys and 110 girls.

At the beginning of the study, 83.2 percent of the UP children and 90 percent of the AP children lived in formally complete families — 13.2 percent of the UP and

8.2 percent of the AP women were divorced, 1.8 percent and 1.8 percent were widowed, and 1.8 percent and 0.0 percent were unmarried. However, even these families (with some few exceptions only) could be considered functionally complete because the mothers had regular partners who resided in the home. In the formally complete homes, 10 percent of the UP children had stepfathers, compared to 3.6 percent of the AP children. These differences are not statistically significant.

In sum, the UP study group consists of 220 children born to women twice denied abortion for the same pregnancy, 110 boys and 110 girls, pair-matched with 220 AP control children born to women who had not requested an abortion. The study also involved all the children's mothers and, to a lesser extent, their fathers or father substitutes.

SOCIAL STRUCTURE OF THE UP AND AP FAMILIES

Age of Parents

In both the UP group and the AP control group, the parents' age at the time of the birth of the child under examination was divided into age groups as shown in Table 6.2. The average age of UP mothers was 25.5 years and that of AP mothers 25.9 years; the age of UP fathers was 29.1 years and that of AP fathers 29.7 years.

Table 6.2. Age of UP and AP parents at child's birth

| Age | UP | | AP | |
	Mothers %	Fathers %	Mothers %	Fathers %
−19	10.9	4.6	7.3	0.5
20−24	38.6	17.1	33.2	17.4
25−29	24.6	35.4	35.4	35.5
30−34	18.2	22.6	18.6	26.5
35−39	7.7	14.3	5.0	13.7
40+	−	6.0	0.5	6.4
Total	100.0	100.0	100.0	100.0

Family Status and Stability

The family status of mothers and fathers was ascertained at the time of the investigation, as shown in Table 6.3. The family status of the mothers, in terms of completeness or incompleteness of the family, was used as a matching criterion. Eight years after the birth of their child, the group of AP mothers contained practically no

58

unmarried women, and only a few divorced women or women married to a man other than the father of their child. The group of UP mothers included a smaller number of married women and a greater number of unmarried women than would correspond to the expected frequencies.

Table 6.3. Family status of mothers and fathers at the time of research (8 years after the birth of the examined child)

Family Status	Mothers		Fathers	
	UP %	AP %	UP %	AP %
Unmarried	1.8	0.0	0.4	0.4
Married to the child's father/mother	73.2	86.4	75.3	86.8
Married to another man/woman	10.0	3.6	11.7	3.2
Divorced	13.2	8.2	10.3	7.8
Widowed/died	1.8	1.8	2.3	1.8
Total	100.0	100.0	100.0	100.0

Among the natural fathers of the examined children, 11.7 percent of UP fathers and 3.2 percent of AP fathers were married to a woman other than the child's mother; 10.3 percent of UP fathers and 7.6 percent of AP fathers were divorced; one father in each sample had remained single (0.4 %); 2.3 percent of UP fathers and 1.8 percent of AP fathers had died.

The stability of the family environment was evaluated from the time of both the child's conception and birth for both groups (Table 6.4). The changes in marital status include marriages, divorces, and remarriages. While more changes occurred among UP mothers — the difference did not reach statistical significance. More specifically, following the birth of the study child, 42 UP mothers divorced (two of them twice), while only 25 AP mothers (none twice) divorced. Among women who had been married to the child's father prior to the birth of the child, 28 divorces were recorded in the UP group and 15 divorces in the AP group. The differences are on the boundary of statistical significance ($p < .06$).

Table 6.4. Number of changes in the family status of UP and AP mothers ($a =$ from the child's conception, $b =$ from the child's birth)

Number of Changes	UP Mothers		AP Mothers	
	a %	b %	a %	b %
No change	61.4	75.0	72.7	84.6
1 change	28.2	18.2	20.0	11.4
2 changes	7.3	5.9	5.5	4.0
3 and more changes	3.1	0.9	1.8	0.0
Total	100.0	100.0	100.0	100.0

Education

In Czechoslovakia, parental educational attainment is the most significant indicator of a family's cultural level. The distribution of education in both samples roughly corresponded to the distribution in Prague, with a somewhat lesser representation of those who had completed general secondary education or graduated from universities.

As shown in Table 6.5, differences in the level of education attained by both women and men were statistically insignificant in both the UP and the AP samples. The basic cultural homogeneity (man's education times woman's education) was high in both the samples.

Table 6.5 The highest education level attained by women and men (at the time of research, 8 years after the child's birth)

Education Level	Women		Men	
	UP %	AP %	UP %	AP %
Basic education				
unskilled workers	28.1	20.0	5.7	6.0
skilled workers	22.0	26.6	41.4	44.5
Lower vocational education	11.9	16.7	5.2	7.4
Completed secondary education	32.5	30.2	31.5	22.7
University education	5.5	6.5	16.2	19.4
Total	100.0	100.0	100.0	100.0

Table 6.6. Basic social groups in terms of the employment and qualification of the mother's partner (at the time of research)

Social Group	UP Families %	AP Families %
I	53.4	53.2
II	34.8	30.1
III	11.8	16.7
Total	100.0	100.0

For purposes of international comparison, the occupational structure of the two samples can be broken into three principal groups in relation to the education and qualification required (around 1970):

    I. Workers and employees engaged in services requiring basic education or lower level vocational education with or without serving an apprenticeship.

60

II. Technical employees, administrative workers, and civil servants, generally requiring completion of secondary (vocational or general) education, or lower vocational education in exceptional circumstances.

III. Specialized professional workers, usually requiring university graduation, or, in some cases, secondary vocational education.

These groups cannot be compared according to income; there are bottom and top limits in each, with average incomes essentially balanced. Yet, they differ in their life-styles, in their life values and goals, and also in nonworking-time interests, even if these differences are gradually diminishing. As noted in Table 6.6, differences in the basic social structure of the two samples are not statistically significant.

Financial Situation of the Families

As regards basic incomes, no substantial differences between the two samples were found to exist in the separate income groups; this concerns both women and men. Compared with national averages, the averages of families in the UP sample (and because of pairing, also in the AP sample) are somewhat lower, clustered predominantly within the medium ranges. A worsening of the family's general financial situation in the course of the past three years was reported by 15 percent of UP families and by 17 percent of AP families. An improvement was mentioned for 40 percent of UP families and 42 percent of AP families, while for the remainder income level remained unchanged.

Number of Children Living in the Family

The average number of children was 2.12 in the UP families and 2.02 in the AP families. At the time of research, the children's average age was 8 years and 5 months in UP families, compared with 8 years and 4 months in AP families. As shown in Table 6.7, most families have two children. In Czechoslovakia, this number is usually considered optimal both with regard to the satisfaction of the parents'

Table 6.7. Number of children living in the family (8 years after the birth of the examined child)

Number of Children	UP Families %	AP Families %
1	22.7	17.3
2	50.4	69.1
3	22.3	10.0
4 or more	4.6	3.6
Total	100.0	100.0

desires and for rearing children. It was thus not easy to find among the AP mothers adequate counterparts to the 50 UP mothers with an unwanted only child; the same difficulty applied to the 59 UP mothers with three or more children.

In pair-matching, greater stress was placed upon the birth order of each child. As apparent in Table 6.8, no statistically significant differences appear between the two samples on birth order.

Table 6.8. Siblings of the examined child

Number of Siblings	In UP Families %	In AP Families %
No siblings	22.7	17.3
1 elder sibling	40.9	47.7
2 elder siblings	8.6	6.8
3 or more elder siblings	3.2	2.7
Younger siblings only	24.6	25.5
Total	100.0	100.0

Housing Situation

In Czechoslovakia, and particularly in Prague, it is of major importance for the life of the young family to have its own flat. This factor has always been taken into consideration in evaluating an application for an interruption of pregnancy. A great many applications (36 %) substantiated their application on the basis of unsatisfactory housing conditions.

At the time of birth of their child, 53 percent of UP parents and 61 percent of AP parents lived in their own flat. Married couples not possessing their own flat mostly shared a flat with the parents of one of the partners. In the interview, 70 per-cent of UP mothers and 73 percent of AP mothers declared themselves to be con-tent, for the time being, with their existing housing conditions.

From the general characterization of the socioeconomic situation of both sam-ples, it can be inferred that no conspicuous differences existed on the indicators of socioeconomic status. In view of the pair-matching, the intervening influence of ex-ternal factors (or of their difference), which might affect the development of the relationship between the mother and her involuntarily born child, was reduced to a minimum. It was also apparent, however, that UP families were less stable than AP families, if stability is evaluated according to the number of changes of the mothers' family status, particularly in the course of the children's life up to age nine.

REASONS FOR ABORTION REQUESTS AND DENIALS

Abortion applications can be divided into two groups, those conforming to the health and social reasons stipulated by the legislation and other than legal reasons presented by the pregnant women in the hope of persuading the commissions to approve their requests. Applications based on health considerations had to be supported by medical diagnoses. As shown in Table 6.9, social reasons appeared most frequently among the denied applications, e.g., housing problems, financial difficulties, and out-of-wedlock pregnancies. In more than two thirds of the cases, the appellate commission denied the woman's appeal because the stated reasons were considered insufficient or untrustworthy. For a large proportion, the pregnancy had continued beyond 12 weeks and termination at that point would have been in violation of the law (Table 6.10).

Table 6.9. Legal justification of applications for an interruption of pregnancy given by UP women

Reasons Given	%
Health reasons	18.4
Advanced age of the woman	0.5
More children in the family	7.1
Disintegration or threatening disintegration of the family	16.0
The woman's economic responsibility for the family	1.4
Unmarried woman	29.3
Financial difficulties of the family	15.0
Housing shortage	36.3

Note: Some applications were substantiated by two reasons, hence the total exceeds 100 percent.

Tabele 6.10. Reasons for the final denial of the application for an interruption of pregnancy

Reasons Given	%
Insufficient reasons	64.6
Pregnancy exceeds 12 weeks	28.6
Only 6 months since the last interruption	8.0
Health contraindications	2.3

Note: Some applications were denied for two reasons, hence the total exceeds 100 percent.

Gynecological examination indicated that almost 70 percent of the women submitted their applications in time, that is, before the end of the tenth week. Those who took longer to reach a decision ran the risk that commission proceedings might last beyond two weeks and thus exceed the legal time limit permitted for interruption of pregnancy on request. Nearly all the applications submitted between the tenth and twelfth weeks, along with those submitted later, were denied.

HYPOTHESES AND DATA

Hypotheses

The basic hypothesis of this study is that there are differences between children born from explicitly unwanted pregnancies and children born from accepted pregnancies. The direction of these differences is to the disadvantage of children born from unwanted pregnancies and should be apparent in their medical history, social integration, educational achievement, psychological condition, and family relations.

More specifically, it was hypothesized that some kind of maladaptation would be more frequent among the UP children and that some undesirable traits would arise, especially in the social interaction of the child with the family, at school, and among peers. It was also hypothesized that unsatisfactory relationships between the mothers and their marital partners would be more common than usual in the UP group, reflecting a negative attitude toward the male sex. That, together with the widely accepted concept that boys are more vulnerable to adverse social-environmental conditions than girls, led to the prediction that male children would suffer relatively more than female children.

It was understood from the beginning that although the UP group was selected on the basis of unwantedness before birth, many of the UP children were likely to become accepted, or indeed loved, after they were born. This expectation was fostered by the observation that those women most determined not to give birth had avoided doing so, while some others had given up their children for adoption or permanent placement in the care of others. Thus, extreme cases of unwantedness had probably been excluded from the sample. The UP children studied are those living with mothers who complied with the decisions of the appellate abortion commissions and accepted the consequences. For children of mothers who continued to have negative feelings, it was hypothesized that manifestations of rejection and overcompensation would appear within the group and that group differences might be more apparent in the distribution of variables than in overall averages.

Naturally, the question arises whether differences between the UP and AP samples are likely to diminish or widen over time. Considering that the UP study group is not at the extreme negative end of the wantedness/unwantedness continuum and that the children are living mostly in complete families, it would be reasonable to assume a gradual ebbing away of unfavorable characteristics. Conversely, the theory of psychological deprivation (*Langmeier* and *Matějček*, 1975) predicts some measure of permanence in psychological disorders due to lack of suitable stimulation in the early developmental stages, even a certain risk of passing these disorders along to the next generation. It was decided to leave this question open at the beginning of the study. An answer is sought in the 20-year follow-up data becoming available (as discussed in the next chapter). A final answer can be given only after most of the UP children have had children of their own and these children move beyond the boundaries of their families in the process of their socialization.

Data Collection at Age Nine

The 220 UP and 220 pair-matched AP children were thoroughly examined at about age nine by members of a research team who did not know (and still do not know for certain) which child belonged to what group. For each child, the researchers collected psychological, sociological, medical, and educational records, plus psychological and sociological data based on interviews with the children themselves, their parents, their teachers, and their peers. Many aspects of child development and parent-child relationships were covered. Sources of data about the children include delivery, pediatric clinic, and school health service records; the child's case history (drawn from interviews with the mother by an experienced social worker and a psychiatrist); an extensive physical examination of the child by an experienced pediatrician; and a psychological examination of the child by a clinical psychologist.

The following psychological assessment measures were used: the Wechsler Intelligence Scale for Children (WISC test); the Bene-Anthony Test of Family Relations; Aspiration-Frustration Test; the child's drawing of his/her family; story completion test; a structured interview focused on the child's relationship with his/her family; a sociogram done in the child's classroom to obtain perceptions of his/her social characteristics; a rating scale for personality traits familiar to those who know the child well (but difficult to elicit in direct psychological investigation), completed independently by each child's mother and teacher; and a rating scale to assess the child's behavior during psychological testing.

Information about the mothers was drawn from the original request for abortion (by the UP women); prenatal and delivery records; a case history interview with the mother based on a 56-item model conducted by a social worker; a structured interview with the mother conducted by a psychiatrist, based on a specially designed questionnaire with scaled questions; and a series of standardized questionnaires and tests completed by the mother under supervision. These included the Czech "Aims in Life" Questionnaire and a supplement called the "H2" Questionnaire; the Eysenck Personality Inventory of Neuroticism and Extraversion; and the Bene-Anthony Test of Family Relations, modified for the parents. In addition, scales were completed independently by the social worker and the psychiatrist to assess the mother's attitude during the interview regarding her family, honesty of response, intelligence, cooperation, and several other qualities (e.g., *Matějček, Dytrych,* and *Schüller,* 1978a). Details are provided in Chapter 10.

Data Analyses

Initial data analysis was divided into two stages (suggested by *Herbert L. Friedman* and *Raymond L. Johnson*). The first stage consisted of inspecting data obtained from a randomly selected subsample of 100 pair-matched children. Comparisons were made of frequency distributions and of means and variances. No statistical tests were performed. On the basis of these initial observations, some of the general hypotheses delineated at the very beginning of the study were elaborated into more specific statements. These hypotheses were then checked in the second stage of the analysis, using the 120 pairs of children not included in the first-stage analysis. However, for the purposes of this report only figures for the entire cohort will be presented.

The significance of differences between samples was measured by means of t-test, chi-square test, the McNemar test, and, in some instances, by correlation coefficients. As one of the hypotheses assumed greater sex differences in the UP population than in the "normal" population, a statistical test of sex by unwantedness interaction was indicated. Three contrasts for differences between sexes, samples, and their interaction were taken as independent variables in the regression analysis, the point of interest being the interaction effect.

For the analysis of rating scales and scaled items in case histories, interviews, school questionnaires, etc., the chi-square test for paired differences seemed most suitable as a modification to the McNemar test.

To eliminate randomly significant differences that may occur if statistical tests are applied to a large number of variables, only a few "critical" items were selected for each hypothesis and predictions made on the basis of theoretical reasoning and clinical experience. Only these items were then used to test the hypotheses; other findings were considered "supplementary."

FINDINGS AT AGE NINE

Early Development

UP mothers cared significantly less for their pregnancies. They registered later in Pregnancy Care Medical Centers and visited them less frequently ($p < .001$). However, comparison of the UP sample and the AP sample shows the latter to have had significantly more complications during pregnancy ($p < .05$) and the puerperal period ($p < .05$). This difference may have resulted from the higher incidence of mothers within the AP sample who very much wanted a child, sought treatment for sterility, or had a more risk-prone, medically sustained pregnancy, etc. However, there were no differences between the two groups in the rates of preterm and postterm deliveries, delivery duration, delivery complications, marked or minimal signs of brain dysfunction, or in the rates of congenital malformations, diagnosed in thorough physical examination (Table 6.11). There were also no differences in birth weight and birth length, with means of 3,358 g and 50.10 cm among the UP children and 3,389 g and 50.13 cm among the AP children.

Thus, the physical health of the children, according to the delivery records and postnatal pediatric records, did not differ in any significant way. This finding suggests that the physical start to life was the same for children of both groups, with the slight differences noted favoring the UP children. Moreover, there is no evidence that the mental condition of the UP mothers and their rejecting attitude toward the pregnancy were manifest in any negative way at the time of birth. However, as shown in Table 6.12, breast-feeding, one of the first objective indicators of the

Table 6.11. Prenatal and perinatal complications and some pediatric findings in UP and AP children

	UP %	AP %
Complications of pregnancies		
no complications at all	73.9	65.3
minor	17.6	19.6
serious	8.5	15.1
paired chi^2 / p	5.9 / < 0.5	
Delivery		
in term	84.9	86.4
preterm or postterm	15.1	13.6
paired chi^2 / p	0.087 / n. s.	
Complications at delivery		
were some	11.4	13.1
no complications	88.6	86.9
paired chi^2 / p	0.091 / n.s.	
Complications during puerperium		
were some	9.2	17.0
no complications	90.8	83.0
paired chi^2 / p	3.769 / < .05	
Congenital malformations		
absent	59.5	61.8
present	40.5	38.2
paired chi^2 / p	0.24 / n.s.	
Minimal brain dysfunction		
absent	70.4	74.5
mild symptoms	25.5	22.3
marked symptoms	4.1	3.2
paired chi^2 / p	1.00 / n.s.	
Impairments of vision		
absent	80.9	81.4
present	19.1	18.6
paired chi^2 / p	0.01 / n.s.	
Impairments of audition		
absent	99.0	98.1
present	1.0	1.9
paired chi^2 / p	0.66 / n.s.	

psychosocial mother-child relationship, is unfavorable for the UP children, despite the significantly higher incidence of puerperium complications in the AP mothers. More UP than AP children were either not breast-fed or breast-fed for only a short time.

During their first eight years, the UP children received medical care for acute illness more frequently than the AP ones ($p < .05$), but there were no differences in the incidence of long-term illness, accidents, operations, or hospitalizations. The UP children also showed a slight but consistent tendency to overweight throughout their development (measured at ages 3, 6, and about 9), while their height did not differ from that of the AP controls or Prague norms. This finding is strikingly similar to that found (in even stronger form) in large samples of children living in children's homes and other institutions of permanent group care (*Langmeier* and *Matějček*, 1975).

Table 6.12. Breast-feeding of UP and AP children

Breast-Feeding	UP %	AP %
Less than 2 weeks	20.0	11.7
3–8 weeks	34.6	48.7
9–12 weeks	34.7	22.5
More than 12 weeks	10.7	17.1
chi^2 / df / p	10.89 / 3 / < .025	

Psychological Development

The UP mothers more frequently described their children as being naughty, stubborn, and bad-tempered at preschool age than did the AP mothers; the difference on bad temper was significant at $p < .05$. There were no apparent differences in UP and AP children's adaptation to the educational process in school. However, UP mothers remembered more often than AP mothers that their children had rejected their new teacher ($p < .01$). At the time of assessment, i.e., in the third grade, more UP than AP children disliked school ($p < .01$).

The UP children were rated significantly lower in diligence in school by their teachers ($p < .05$). Although not statistically significant, the UP children tended to show less concentration, initiative, and tidiness than the AP children. Mothers and teachers, independently, rated their children on 11 personal characteristics. Both rated the UP children significantly more excitable ($p < .05$ and $p < .01$, respectively). Also, on all the other characteristics except "demandingness," the mean ratings of both mothers and teachers were lower for the UP children than for the AP controls.

As shown in Table 6.13, both groups of children obtained similar mean scores on the WISC: total scores of 102.4 for UP children and 103.3 for the AP controls. Teachers' assessment of behavior and performance at school was, however, less favorable for the UP children. In school subjects, as measured by the most recent grades, the UP children scored lower than the AP controls. The sharpest difference was in the grade for the Czech language ($p < .05$), a skill particularly representative of the child's socio-emotional environment. However, little difference was noted in grades on arithmetic, which under normal conditions correlates most with the general level of intelligence.

Table 6.13. Performance of UP and AP children on the Wechsler Intelligence Scale for Children

	UP		AP		
	Mean	SD	Mean	SD	*t*-test
Verbal score	101.45	10.63	102.44	11.72	0.93 n.s.
Performance score	102.83	13.40	103.66	13.28	0.66 n.s.
Total score	102.44	11.11	103.28	11.83	0.77 n.s.

Peer Relations

On the sociometric scales, the UP children as a group were significantly more often "rejected as friend" by their schoolmates than the AP control children ($p < .05$). They were also consistently ascribed less desirable social characteristics in all other

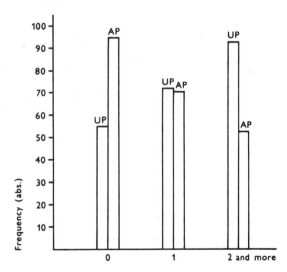

Fig. 6.1. Sociometric examination of UP and AP children.

69

sociometric measures, although not significantly so. If high scores are considered separately, some the differences become more pronounced. For example, more children in the UP sample collected more than six votes as the greatest "coward" in school class ($p < .025$), as the most "audacious" ($p < .025$), and as the most "clowning and showing off " ($p < .01$).

The unfavorable position of the UP children among their classmates becomes more marked if the cumulative effect is considered. Eight sociometric measures were chosen as "hard" indicators of maladjustment of a child in his or her peer group: not to be chosen as a friend by any other child, to be rejected as a friend by six or more classmates, to be considered by six or more classmates as the greatest coward, braggart, loner, most audacious, funniest (clowning and showing off), or by at least ten classmates as "fighting a lot." As shown in Table 6.14, significantly more UP children than AP controls were rejected or disrespected by their classmates for two or more negative traits ($p < .001$).

Table 6.14. Percentage of UP and AP children exhibiting maladjustment traits on sociometric examination

	UP %	AP %
No maladjustment traits	25.0	43.2
One maladjustment trait	32.7	32.3
Two or more maladjustment traits	42.3	24.5
chi^2 / df / p	21.02 / 2 / < .001	

Utilization of Intelligence

Although there was no difference in aspiration between the groups on the Aspiration-Frustration Test, the behavior of the UP children in the face of frustration

Table 6.15. Some results on Aspiration-Frustration Test

	UP	AP
Aspiration minus achievement Fifth attempt, i.e., first after frustration		
Average	4.55	5.03
SD	3.11	3.43
t-test = 1.56 p = n.s.		
Aspiration minus achievement Eighth attempt, i.e., fourth after frustration		
Average	3.31	2.54
SD	3.92	3.15
t-test = 2.25 p = < .025		

was significantly less adaptive ($p < .05$) (Table 6.15). When not permitted to achieve more than half their previous performance, after four unsuccessful trials, the UP children lowered their aspiration by hardly a quarter on average, whereas the AP controls lowered their aspirations by half. Adaptation to frustration is usually correlated with intelligence. This was the case with the AP control children ($p < .01$), whereas it was not so for the UP children, who were not taking advantage of their intelligence in this demanding situation. They were also rated consistently (although not significantly) lower on intelligence by their mothers, teachers, and classmates, despite the lack of objective differences as measured by the intelligence tests. In general, the UP boys showed the poorest adaptability to stress ($p < .025$).

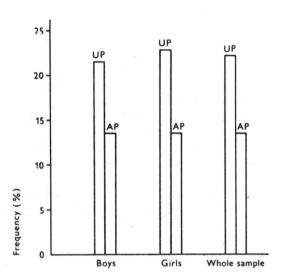

Fig. 6.2. Aspiration-Frustration Test in UP and AP children.

Child's Own Assessment of Psychosocial Situation

It was assumed that projective and semiprojective tests applied to children of both groups would differentiate distinctly between them. Surprisingly, the Bene-Anthony Projective Test of Family Relations did not show any significant group variances. The other measures employed (Family Drawings, Story Completion Test, structured interview with the child) also showed only a few significant differences. But even the few that emerged were unfavorable for the UP children. (As these were not among "critical items" selected in advance, they were not further interpreted.)

Generally speaking, the findings suggest that the UP children do not see their family psychosocial and emotional situation as deviant, at least not sufficiently

71

stressful to emerge as such on the psychological methods employed. It should be remembered that the children were examined around nine years of age, i.e., a period preceding the development of introspection. Moreover, projective tests used in related studies with deprived children of similar age residing in children's homes yielded "meager" and unconvincing results, although the children's psychosocial behavior was evidently deviant and detectable by other methods (*Langmeier* and *Matějček*, 1975).

Sex Differences

Boys and girls appeared to differ on many variables within both samples. The question is, however, whether there are some specific differences unfavorable to UP boys when compared with the AP boys and with the girls of both samples. The answer may be drawn from interactional analysis of sex by wantedness.

Interactional analysis shows that gender differences are practically absent from ratings completed by teachers on individual items in sociograms performed by schoolmates. Important differences between the sexes were noted in the mothers' perceptions and judgments. Unlike the UP girl, the UP boy is disproportionately (i.e., significantly) more frequently considered by his mother to be "naughty" ($p < .05$) and "disobedient" ($p < .05$) at preschool age, less intelligent ($p < .05$), and less egotistic ($p < .05$), i.e. specifically "buying" interest and favor of other children by small gifts, services, etc.

There were no differences in breast-feeding, but significantly more of the UP boys than the AP boys suffered from long-term illnesses (33.0 % and 18.5 %, respectively), while there was almost nothing to distinguish between the UP and AP girls in this variable.

Findings Relating to UP and AP Mothers

From the multitude of data relating to the mothers, fathers, and families, only those having immediate bearing on the psychosocial development of the child were selected for study. Pair-mathing of AP with UP mothers precluded disparities on

Table 6.16. Unfavorable hereditary factors in mothers' histories

	UP %	AP %
"Mental"	43.0	37.6
"Somatic"	57.0	62.4
chi^2 / df / p	0.84 / 1 / n.s.	

72

the basic demographic variables and provided the opportunity to compare both samples on mostly sociopsychological indicators.

Case histories failed to support the suggestion that the rejecting attitude to the pregnancy might be connected to deeper familial pathology. As shown in Table 6.16, the past histories of the mothers in both groups included the occurrence of mental retardation, treated mental disorders, nervous diseases, neurotic complaints, alcoholism, suicides, somatic conditions due to hereditary factors, sensory defects, malformations, etc.

No differences between the groups were noted in questionnaire items relating to the mother's own childhood (e.g., how "happy" the mother's childhood was, who was the leading figure in her childhood, how sociable she was, what the mother's first loves in adolescence were like, etc.). The only point to emerge was that the UP mothers had slightly fewer siblings than the AP mothers had (paired $chi^2 = 3.89$; $p < .05$).

No significant differences were apparent from tests of mothers' personality traits and value systems, which were administered and assessed in a standard way. Also, there were no differences in the families' economic situation (the mothers' and fathers' incomes, income per capita, etc.), housing conditions, or cultural-social level (measured by interests, use of leisure time, etc.) when rated by the mothers themselves.

As shown in Table 6.4, the UP families were less stable. Following the birth of the child, the UP mothers more frequently had a "change in family status" due to divorce (21 %) than the AP mothers (12 %). Although the difference is statistically significant ($p < .025$), it is so small that, as will be noted, it cannot be regarded as decisive for the deviations in the psychological development of the UP children.

Table 6.17. Number of abortions in childbirth records and in case histories

Number of Abortions Stated in Childbirth Records	UP %	AP %
None	72.4	81.1
One	19.5	13.3
Two	5.2	4.7
Three or more	2.9	0.9
chi^2 / df / p	5.61 / 3 / n.s.	

Number of Abortions Given in Case Histories	UP %	AP %
None	57.3	63.5
One	25.0	23.7
Two	10.2	10.9
Three or more	7.5	1.9
chi^2 / df / p	7.70 / 3 / n.s.	

It was hypothesized that UP mothers were more likely than AP mothers to have had induced abortions, both before and after the delivery of the unwanted child. Although the total number of abortions showed no significant difference between the two groups, there were some striking differences nonetheless. A history of three or more abortions was mentioned four times more often among the UP women than among the AP controls (8 % compared with 2 %) (Table 6.17).

If the indicators of the "external" state of the family showed no, or only very slight, differences between the groups, the picture becomes quite different when internal relationships are examined.

First there were the findings of the research social workers who visited the families, repeatedly talked to the mothers, prepared the case histories, and eventually made their ratings on the standard eight-item scales. (None of them, of course, knew who belonged to which group.) Three of these eight items significantly differentiated between the groups – the UP mothers knew less about their child and could provide less information ($p < .025$); they showed a less warm relationship towards the child (paired chi^2 = 11.68; $p < .001$); but they behaved with greater self-assurance ($p < .05$).

Also, the class teachers who viewed the family through the child and assessed it on a four-item scale could see no differences between the groups on the "cultural level of the family." However, regarding the "internal life of the family," they found

Table 6.18. Internal family atmosphere in UP and AP families

	UP %	AP %
Assessment of mother by social worker:		
Attitude to husband		
definitely negative (rejecting)	12.2	4.5
positive or mildly negative	87.8	95.5
chi^2 / df / p	6.77 / 1 / < .01	
Assessment of mother by psychiatrist:		
Attitude to husband		
definitely negative (rejecting)	14.7	8.3
positive or midly negative	85.3	91.7
chi^2 / df / p	4.24 / 1 / < .05	
Mother considers her marriage as:		
very happy	6.7	5.1
average	69.8	70.7
less happy	9.1	17.2
definitely unhappy	14.4	7.0
chi^2 / df / p	11.19 / 3 / < .025	
Worries and troubles which accompanied the birth of child:		
no worries at all	30.3	53.4
financial and housing	19.8	15.5
disharmony in marital life	12.6	5.3
child's health	10.2	7.3
other worries	27.1	18.5
chi^2 / df / p	24.40 / 4 / < .001	

74

	UP %	AP %
Assessment of family by teacher		
Cultural level of family		
(5-point scale, 1 — lowest)		
mean rating	3.15	3.25
SD	0.60	0.60
paired chi^2 / p	2.84 / n.s.	
Internal family life		
(4-point scale, 1 — lowest)		
mean rating	3.18	3.37
SD	1.07	0.93
paired chi^2 / p	1.57 / n.s.	
Care of child		
(5-point scale, 1 — lowest)		
mean rating	3.45	3.65
SD	0.79	0.81
paired chi^2 / p	5.54 / < .05	
Cooperation with school		
(4-point scale, 1 — lowest)		
mean rating	2.77	2.92
SD	0.55	0.44
paired chi^2 / p	9.38 / < .01	
Assessment of mother by social worker		
(4-point scale, 1 — lowest)		
Mother informed about child		
mean of ratings	2.82	2.93
SD	0.64	0.55
paired chi^2 / p	5.19 / < .02	
Mother's positive attitude to child		
mean of ratings	2.91	3.08
SD	0.52	0.47
paired chi^2 / p	11.88 / < .001	

differences unfavorable to the UP families in the "care of the child" and "family-school cooperation" at the level of $p < .05$ and $p < .01$, respectively (Tables 6.18 and 6.19).

The UP mothers themselves viewed their present marriage as less happy on average ($p < .025$). The social workers on their visits to the families and the psychiatrist during individual interviews more often rated the UP women's attitude toward their husbands as negative ($p < .01$ and $p < .05$, respectively.)

What is, however, of particular interest in this connection is the mother's attitude to the child. The UP mothers twice requested termination of this pregnancy. How did they perceive this circumstance some nine years later when asked directly at the very end of the psychiatric interview? And how did they interpret the fathers' attitude in retrospect?

As apparent in Table 6.20, 38 percent of the UP mothers denied having ever been before an abortion commission; indeed, some even said that they had planned the pregnancy and were greatly looking forward to it. The UP mothers were thus divided into those who denied their rejecting attitude toward the pregnancy (N = 83) and those who admitted it (N = 137).

Table 6.20. Mother's and father's attitude toward pregnancy

The pregnancy was:	Mothers		Fathers	
	UP %	AP %	UP %	AP %
Strongly wanted and planned	5.9	35.2	10.0	38.5
Wanted although unplanned	7.7	23.7	7.8	24.8
Neutrally accepted	14.5	32.4	20.5	26.6
Unwanted, but accepted	9.5	8.7	11.4	8.7
Unwanted, rejected (abortion applied for)	62.4	0.0	50.2	1.4

As for the fathers' attitudes, the overwhelming majority of UP mothers reported it as being the same as theirs: rejection of this pregnancy was a joint decision by both parents. A joint rejecting attitude was reported by 94 mothers, while a joint non-rejecting attitude was given by 55 mothers. There remained 70 mothers reporting a discrepancy between their and the fathers' attitudes; 16 claimed that it was the father who did not want the pregnancy to continue, while she (the mother) wished to keep it. Conversely, 42 mothers stated that they did not want the pregnancy, whereas the fathers wanted it to continue, or at least disagreed with the abortion decision. Another 12 mothers mentioned disagreements within a generally positive attitude toward the pregnancy.

Naturally, negative attitudes were absent among the AP controls. There were three cases, however, where the father was in favor of abortion, while the mother was not. In general, though, this group is characterized by greater agreement in the attitudes of both parents. When the mothers did mention some differences, they mostly described their attitudes as less favorable than those of the fathers.

The question arises whether those children whose mothers now deny their originally negative attitude toward their existence develop in some ways differently from the children whose mothers admit the fact of having applied for abortion. We conducted an extensive investigation and checked all the basic indicators of the child's development, including the summarizing Maladaptation Score (described below), and found only quite isolated statistically significant differences. Moreover, these are too variable to yield any meaningful, plausible interpretation. Subsequent detailed examination showed that both "denial" and "admission" may be motivated by various reasons. The overall inclination of the UP women seemed to be to want to "appear in a better light" at the time of interview.

We also failed to uncover any significant differences between the development of children from families where the mother reported her and the father's attitude toward the pregnancy to have been the same and that of children from families where mothers mentioned divergent attitudes. In all likelihood there are a variety of factors at play which make these subgroups quite heterogeneous internally.

In general, the attitude toward the pregnancy appears to be in accordance with the mothers' presentation of their attitudes toward the child born from it. They were replying to questions as to what effect the birth of the child had had on their health, mental condition, economic situation of the family, harmonious relationships between the marital partners, and the relationships within the entire family. Then they summed up all these "effects" in an item called: "The effect of the child's arrival on our family."

As shown in Table 6.21, the UP group includes significantly more of those who stated that they were reluctant to accept the child's birth and that it had an adverse effect on the life of the family. The subsequent development of the mother's relationship with the child had, however, proceeded in such a way as to obliterate any difference between the groups. Accordingly, the mothers of both groups expressed about the same satisfaction with the child.

There was no difference between the groups in the time the children spent outside their own family for one reason or another up to the age of three. Almost the same number of children in each group attended crèche and kindergarten. Although somewhat more children in the UP group spent long periods under their grandparents' care, in infants' homes, or children's homes, the absolute figures are

Table 6.21. Development of the mother's relationship toward the child

	UP %	AP %
The mother accepted the birth of the child under examination		
willingly	29.5	50.2
neutrally	51.4	42.5
reluctantly	19.1	7.3
paired chi^2 / p	21.46 / <.001	
The change produced in the family by the child's birth was		
favorable	38.2	61.8
none at all	48.2	30.0
unfavorable	13.6	8.2
paired chi^2 / p	19.56 / <001	
With the child's increasing age the mother's relationship toward it is		
increasingly better	38.2	35.5
the same as ever	49.5	51.3
increasingly worse	12.3	13.2
paired chi^2 / p	0.90 / n.s.	
Mother's satisfaction with the child at present		
satisfied	50.9	55.4
average	41.8	41.4
dissatisfied	7.3	3.2
paired chi^2 / p	1.96 / n.s.	

so small (never above five) that they cannot be used as an argument. Thus, it is not possible to attribute the later developmental deviations of the UP children to classic psychological deprivation caused by early separation from the family.

However, as shown in Table 6.22, the difference in the grandparents' participation in the upbringing of the UP and AP children is highly significant ($p < .01$). This is in keeping with the common experience that whenever things get out of hand in a family and the emotional situation threatens to become unfavorable for the children, it is up to grandparents to lend a hand. A similar picture emerged in a study of children in families where the father was an alcoholic, when exactly the same methodology was used (*Matějček*, 1981).

Table 6.22. Childrearing in UP and AP families

	UP %	AP %
Childrearing		
in family only	52.7	71.4
also other	47.3	28.6
chi² / df / p	16.22 / 1 / < .003	
Parents shared childrearing with grandparents		
yes	41.4	29.1
no	58.6	70.9
chi² / df / p	7.26 / 1 / < .01	

The findings in Table 6.21, summing up mothers' present attitudes toward the children, are generally optimistic: only a small group of UP children rejected at the outset of pregnancy remain, in their mothers' words, still unaccepted at the end of eight years. (However, this affirmation by the mothers is shown in a different light by the Maladaptation Score, described below.) Notwithstanding the tendency of the UP mothers to distort facts to suit social conventions, most of them must be cred-

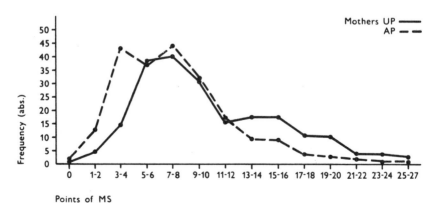

Fig. 6.3. Maladaptation Score (MS) in UP and AP mothers.

78

ited with a significant positive shift in attitudes toward the child, particularly on the conscious level.

An interpretational framework is provided by *Festinger's* cognitive dissonance theory and a special model situation of "forced decision." Women renewing their request for abortion after the first denied application evidently still had enough internal arguments in favor of the attitude "not to have a baby." The final negative decision of the commission necessarily brought a new cognitive dissonance and greatly enhanced tension for them. To reduce this tension means to look for new arguments supporting the forced decision, i.e., not "against the child" any more, but "for the child." This is by no means easy. There were women who would not have the commission's decision forced on them and who achieved the abortion by other means. Those who accepted the commission's decision were most likely to attempt to reduce the tension. The measure of success they achieved probably depended, in large part, on their ability to enlist the help of their parents in the rearing of the UP child and the perceived security of their partner relations.

The UP mothers do not constitute any "special" or "marginal" group of the general population. At the time the child was to be born, they were definitely not threatened by any material deprivation. In later years, they were not "overburdened" by children, having largely one, two, and, at most, three. (A fourth child or more appeared in only ten cases, which is 4.6 %.) They had no hereditary "predisposition," nor did they stand out as a special group in personality features as examined by current psychological tests. However, to social workers and teachers they appeared, in everyday social situations, as problem-prone personalities, with less satisfactory relationships with their immediate social groups, including the child under examination. At the same time, analysis of the findings shows that the group of UP mothers is heterogeneous and that it includes only some vaguely defined types at the very most. UP mothers exhibit a large number of mild deviations, but these are difficult to aggregate under a common denominator.

The main criteria of their relationship to the child and success in the maternal role are, of course, the children themselves. The psychological development and behavior of the children provide more information about the maternal care and emotinal atmosphere in their families than can social workers, teachers, and other external observers.

Maladaptation Score (MS)

Following statistical analyses, additional efforts centered on developing a descriptive indicator of maladaptation. Sixty items were selected from the case history material, questionnaires, and other psychological assessment devices which could be interpreted as providing evidence of maladaptation (MS), indicative of some shortcoming, imperfection, immaturity, or at least problem-proneness in the psychosocial development and social integration of the child. Only hard items were se-

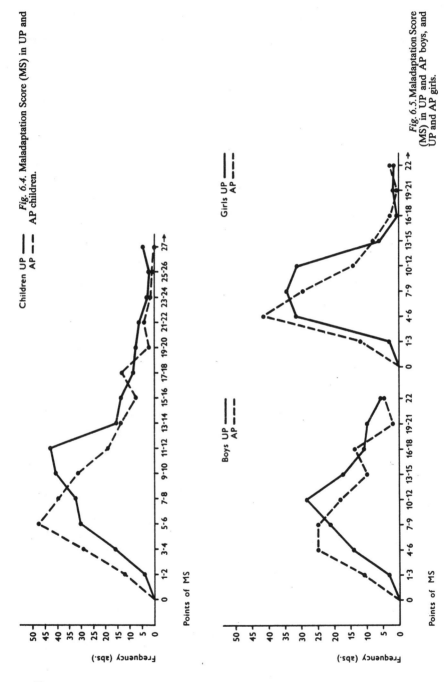

Fig. 6.4. Maladaptation Score (MS) in UP and AP children.

Fig. 6.5. Maladaptation Score (MS) in UP and AP boys, and UP and AP girls.

80

Table 6.23. Maladaptation Score differences between UP and AP children

	N	Average	SD	t-test	p
Group					
UP	220	10.59	5.35	3.86	< .001
AP	220	8.69	4.98		
Boys					
UP	110	12.23	5.93	3.16	< .005
AP	110	9.81	5.42		
Girls					
UP	110	8.95	4.12	2.47	< .025
AP	110	7.56	4.12		
Interaction analysis					
groups UP × AP				4.00	< .001
boys × girls				5.82	< .001
interaction				1.08	n.s.

lected, that is, those showing extreme scores on rating scales, notable differences between high intelligence scores on the WISC and low school performance, high scores of negative traits assessed sociometrically, etc.

Each child's MS was produced by simply summing up his/her "negative points." The higher the number of negative indicators, the more can the child be considered as problem-prone at present and at risk for the future. The mother's maladaptation score was created similarly, based on negative indicators selected from the case histories, structured interviews, questionnaires, and medical records.

As shown in Table 6.23 and Figures 6.4 and 6.5, the UP children had significantly higher maladaptation scores than the AP controls. There were fewer well-adapted UP children and more were slightly or severely maladapted ($p < .001$). The UP boys manifested the highest MS and were generally assessed more negatively than the AP boys. Differences between UP and AP girls were less marked than between the boys but were more unfavorable for the UP than the AP girls. Interaction analysis, controlling simultaneously for wantedness and sex, did not, however, demonstrate that these differences were significant.

Regression Analysis:
Sex/Minimal Brain Dysfunction

When the MS was the dependent variable in a regression analysis with the matching criteria as well as some other measures the independent variables, the sex of the child was found to have the greatest relationship to the child's MS in the group of UP children and the second most significant in the AP control group ($p < .001$). Another significant association with MS among the UP children was evidence of minimal brain dysfunction (damage to the central nervous system) as

Table 6.24. Regression coefficients and their significance within the set of "independent" variables. The child's Maladaptation Score is a dependent variable. Comparison of UP children and AP (control) children.

	UP children			AP children		
	Coef. of Regression	t-test of Regression	p	Coef. of Regression	t-test of Regression	p
Mother's Maladaptation Score	.240	2.640	< .01	.439	4.754	< .001
Sex	−3.137	−4.468	< .001	−2.646	−4.026	< .001
Mother's age	−.695	−1.897	−	−.203	−.583	−
Mother's education	.195	.789	−	.163	.719	−
Family stability	−1.114	−1.534	−	.103	.121	−
Number of children	.847	1.874	−	.279	.551	−
Own father	.913	.706	−	−2.284	−1.606	−
Father's education	−.064	−.251	−	.035	.151	−
Income	.516	1.137	−	−.857	−1.534	−
IQ WISC	−.028	−.780	−	−.042	−1.350	−
Minimal brain dysfunction	1.237	2.708	< 01	.378	.908	−
Mother's attitude to pregnancy	−1.150	−1.656	−	−.322	−.913	−

detected by pediatric examination ($p < .01$) (Table 6.24). This variable did not contribute significantly to the variation in MS among the AP controls, despite the fact that the number of children with minimal brain dysfunction was similar in both groups (30 UP children and 25 AP children). The MS differences among the UP children were statistically very significant ($p < .001$). It appears that minimal brain dysfunction is accentuated in a context of unwanted pregnancy associated with less favorable psychosocial influences, and in a less propitious emotional home atmosphere. Even its milder forms come to the surface more than would be the case with such a child living in an otherwise normal home atmosphere.

Mothers

The mothers' MS was the third most important variable in relation to the child's MS in the UP group and the most important in the AP group. The dispersion of scores among the mothers was similar to that already noted for the children, with differences between UP and AP mothers also statistically significant in disfavor of the UP mothers. It appears that mothers in both groups deemed problem-prone by independent observers are likely to have children who experience greater difficulty in adaptation.

Only Children/Unwanted

One of the most important findings concerns only children in both groups. There were 50 onlies in each sample. The UP only children had the highest MS and the AP onlies the lowest MS, the difference being notably significant ($p < .01$). The possible meaning of this finding is that if a woman had only one child, born from an unwanted pregnancy, the probability of that child's social maladaptation increases significantly. It seems likely that in such cases some sort of maternal role rejection is brought into play, an occurrence which merits further and deeper investigation. Such a finding could serve as an early indicator of a need for special counseling of the children and families concerned.

Other Variables

Less significant findings were noted on other variables. Changes in the mother's family status have a more severe effect on the UP children. To some extent, an AP child may be "protected" from maladaptation by family stability, whereas the UP child is not. The presence of a natural father in the family is a positive factor in the AP group, whereas it is not in the UP group ($p < .02$). However, the presence of a stepfather in the family does not lower the MS in the AP group, whereas it does in the UP children ($p < .02$).

MS Conclusions

In all, four independent variables of those studied were significant predictors of the child's MS: sex, minimal brain dysfunction, mother's maladaptation, and "un-wantedness," i.e., mother's attitude to the pregnancy. No other factor, including the child's intelligence, the mother's age at the time of the birth, the number of children in the family, stability of the family, and presence of an actual father or a stepfather, reached a 5 percent level of significance. This finding renders the rejection of the child at the time of pregnancy a major factor, influencing later personality formation and social functioning, at least insofar as these are reflected in the maladaptation score.

Review of the MS findings also showed that a considerable number of UP children are as well adjusted as their matched AP controls. Nine percent of UP children had scores within the range that could be taken as a good indicator of adaptation, 0 to 4 (the average for the AP controls minus one standard deviation), while 18 percent of the AP controls obtained an MS of 16 or higher (the average plus one standard deviation for the UP group).

As an ad hoc global measure of problem-proneness, the MS indicates that otherwise healthy and intelligent UP children seem, as a group, to become less adaptive, less socially mature, and less prepared to cope with the demands of social life than their AP counterparts. These findings suggest that in the life history of a child, unwanted pregnancy represents something of an "aggravating" factor or circumstance, i.e., a certain risk that may or may not materialize in a particular situation in life. Unwanted pregnancy alone does not specifically harm the child's development, but in its wake come a variety of other factors, which collectively appear to influence the development of the child and his or her social integration.

CONCLUSIONS AT AGE NINE

Initial follow-up at around age nine suggested that involuntary childbearing has varied and sometimes unfavorable consequences for the subsequent life of the child. Although overall differences between the children born following unwanted conception and the matched controls were not dramatic around nine years of age, the observations tended to support many of the major hypotheses. It was suggested that the findings were consonant with a condition identified as psychological subdeprivation (*Langmeier* and *Matějček*, 1975).

There is no evidence that the UP children represent a distinct biological subgroup of the child population. They started life in conditions of physical and mental health similar to those of the AP children, but subsequently were breast-fed for shorter periods, were slightly but consistently overweight, and experienced a higher incidence of acute illness (and of longer duration for boys). While the intelligence of UP and AP children was normal, UP children had lower school grades (especially in the Czech language). Their intellectual capabilities were less apparent in socially demanding situations. They were perceived in terms of lower social status and acceptance by their schoolmates and teachers, and were given specific patterns of negative ratings by their mothers and teachers.

The common denominator that may underlie the differences between UP and AP children on individual variables is that the UP children, particularly the boys, more frequently find it difficult to cope with stress and frustration. This is in accord with general experience: less than satisfactory family interactions provoke more pronounced reactions and less adaptive behavior from boys than from girls. Thus, the UP boys are caught in a vicious circle of interaction. The expectations of parents are repeatedly frustrated. This, in turn, leads to reactions on the part of the child, which then increase the chances for maladaptive behavior in the future.

The maladaptation score further refined and distinguished differences between UP and AP children. In families with children born from unwanted pregnancies, unfavorable factors appear to have a cumulative and perhaps compounding negative effect, resulting in higher maladaptation scores. An only child whose pregnancy was unwanted probably faces the most difficult future, confronted by what appears to be the mother's rejection of the maternal role.

Although only some of the many individual variables examined showed statistically significant differences, the differences were consistent, pointed in the same direction, and were cumulatively impressive. It was also apparent that the differences between the UP and AP children, derived from independently obtained material as well as from direct examination, were not dramatic. No single test, no individual item, and no indicator in the case history was capable by itself of distinguishing the UP children from the AP children so as to enable an experienced clinician to identify an "unwanted" child easily and reliably. It should be recalled, however, that the extreme cases of "unwantedness" in the original population of mothers twice denied abortion (those culminating in illegal pregnancy termination or separation from the child after birth) were not included in the sample.

The basic psychological needs of the UP children were met less satisfactorily than those of the AP children. The early and vigorous tendency of UP children to seek gratification and to assert themselves strongly motivates a certain behavioral pattern, which the given situation systematically reinforces, so that it becomes a more or less permanent feature. One may hypothesize that this process originated in the asynchronous interaction of mother and child from the very beginning, maybe even before birth (as evident, for example, in the significantly less amount of breast-feeding in the UP group and the UP mother's dissatisfacion with the economic and emotional circumstances surrounding the childbirth).

The unconditional acceptance of the child by the mother is the essential prerequisite for an effective mutual psychological interaction. In the case of children born from unwanted pregnancies, and included in the Prague study, the relationship is not that of direct rejection of the child by his/her mother and family (which is the exception), resulting in an actual or psychoemotional abandonment of the child (recall the continuum of wantedness-unwantedness of the child). Rather, acceptance is incomplete, ineffective, and ambivalent, leading to more or less deviant interactions, less maternal empathy with the child's needs, less understanding of his/her behavioral signals, less warm emotional interchange of stimuli, etc. This may then give rise to a clinical picture (detectable in the sample of UP children as a whole) that approaches the classical picture of psychological deprivation, to be found in children growing up in the emotional poverty of an institutional environment. In the case of unwantedness, the picture takes on a subdued and less dramatic appearance. That is why we have called it "subdeprivation." Yet, we believe it to be no less real or specific.

Subdeprivation fits with the complex of small deviations from normal mental development which are of growing social consequence today. Outwardly, it is relatively less conspicuous — still, it is probably a more serious and more dangerous deficit for society than, for example, slightly below-average intellect or minimal brain dysfunction. The effects of subdeprivation most probably affect the personality more deeply and may even be transmitted to the next generation, a hypothesis to be explored in the future.

In sum, the findings around age nine suggested that a woman's originally rejecting attitude toward her pregnancy does not inevitably lead to behavioral difficulties in the child. The belief that every child unwanted during pregnancy remains unwanted is not necessarily true. It is equally untrue that the birth of an originally unwanted child causes a complete change in maternal attitude. Not every woman who becomes a mother will love her child. The child of a woman denied abortion appears to be born into a potentially handicapping situation. At the same time, some factors in the life of mother and child have a positive impact. Further observations seemed essential for a clearer understanding of the longer-term effects of unwantedness during pregnancy and are discussed in the next chapter.

Chapter 7

The Prague Cohort: Adolescence and Early Adulthood

Zdeněk Dytrych, Zdeněk Matějček, and Vratislav Schüller

Background

When the Prague Cohort was about 14 years of age, it became possible to search the records of the child psychiatric and school counseling centers in Prague. Fortythree UP children (31 boys and 12 girls) and 30 AP children (18 boys and 12 girls) had come to the attention of these facilities. All referrals had been made independently of the research project. The professional staff examining the UP and the AP children were entirely unaware of their status as participants in a longitudinal study.

Review of the case records showed that, although differences in number of referrals were slight, the UP children were seen significantly more often because of serious behavior disorders requiring therapeutic treatment. The AP children had been referred for comparatively less serious developmental problems or irregularities that required primarily administrative actions, e.g., referral to special schools, delayed school entrance, or remedial treatment of specific learning disabilities.

Follow-Up Inquiries

The findings at age 14 further stimulated the decision to conduct a follow-up study when the children had become young adolescents between 14 and 16 years of age. In 1977, it became possible to locate 216 UP children and 215 AP controls, achieving a 98 percent follow-up rate. This high rate was attained in part because the Central Population Register establishes separate file cards for adolescents on reaching age 15. Another mail questionnaire was dispatched in 1979. A third follow-up was conducted in 1983-84 when the "children" had reached young adulthood and were between 21 and 23 years old. It was possible to reexamine 160 UP subjects (73 percent follow-up) and 155 AP controls (70 percent follow-up). The lower follow-up rate was largely due to absences from Prague, as study participants were in military service or had moved out of the city.

FOLLOW-UP AT AGES 14-16

Data Collection

The 1977 follow-up focused on three areas: the families, the schools, and the children. The questionnaires and rating scales previously used with the families were readministered as before. A questionnaire and a rating scale of "personal qualities" were used in the schools. Each child (now adolescent) was asked to complete the Children's Report of Parental Behavior (CRPBI) developed by *Schludermann* and *Schludermann* (1970). The objective was to assess each adolescent's perception of parental attitudes and behavior.

School Achievement

It will be recalled that there were no differences on the Wechsler Intelligence Scale for Children (WISC) at age nine. While intelligence tests were not repeated at ages 14 to 16, teachers' assessments of intelligence on a rating scale were entirely similar for both groups. However, the school performance of the UP study group continued to deteriorate so much that the difference in overall school achievement between the UP and AP groups reached statistical significance ($p < .05$). The difference was greater between UP and AP boys than between UP and AP girls. The largest difference was noted between those UP and AP children who graduated from nine-year elementary schools and transferred to secondary schools ($chi^2 = 7.08$, $df = 2$; $p < .01$). This finding suggests that under increased school pressure the UP children are even less likely to perform very well. Inspection of the data reveals that the difference is not so much in UP children failing more often but rather in being substantially underrepresented among the students graded above average, very good, or outstanding. This observation was confirmed by teachers' ratings of desirable work abilities. The UP children consistently appeared worse, primarily due to underrepresentation in the above-average categories. Finally, as compared to AP controls, a significantly larger number of UP children did not continue their education to secondary school, but instead became apprentices or started jobs without prior vocational training.

Personal Qualities

Six years eairler, the mothers and teachers had rated the UP children as significantly less conscientious and more excitable. On reassessment with the same rating scales, the picture was essentially the same ($p < .05$ for conscientiousness and $p < .02$ for excitability). In addition, the UP children were now rated as significantly

88

less obedient than the AP controls by their teachers (chi^2 = 9.12, df = 4, $p < .05$) and by their mothers (chi^2 = 12.12, df = 4, $p < .02$). Moreover, from the teacher's perspective, the UP children were seen as either less sociable or more hyperactive than the AP controls (chi^2 = 13.75, df = 4, $p < .01$). The girls were mostly responsible for the difference in sociability. Differences were stronger in children still in elementary school than in those who had graduated to secondary or technical school. The differentiating factor at secondary school was primarily school performance, while it was largely behavior at elementary school.

Perceptions of Parental Attitudes

Six years earlier, no differences were apparent on the Bene-Anthony Test of Family Relations. Both the UP and the AP children had assessed their relationships with their parents and those of their parents with them in the same positive way. Now, in early adolescence, the Children's Report of Parental Behavior (*Schludermanns'* CRPBI) reflected differences when factor analysis was employed to study five parental attitudes in Czechoslovakia: positive interest in the child, hostility, authoritarian attitude, autonomy, and inconsistency in educational practices (*Matějček* and *Říčan*, 1983).

The attitudes of both mothers and fathers were evaluated. Of the 440 possible questionnaires, 213 UP and 220 AP responses were received. The assessment of the fathers was available for 194 UP subjects and 195 AP controls, although a larger number than those missing were no longer living in the home.

Compared to the controls, the UP subjects perceived their mothers as showing significantly less positive maternal interest toward them ($t = 2.03$, $p < .05$). However, there were no differences in perceived hostility. The UP subjects also perceived their mothers as less authoritarian (chi^2 = 17.75, df = 8, $p < .05$) but no differences were noted on autonomy and inconsistency in educational practices. The UP boys particularly perceived their mothers' behavior as either quite nondirective (nonauthoritarian) or else highly authoritarian. The correlation between perceived authoritarian attitude and mother's positive interest is significantly stronger for the AP controls. This may imply that AP controls closely associate parental authority and guidance with parental love and positive feelings. The UP subjects peceived less parental interest and felt either neglected or, conversely, oppressed by parental authority. Symptomatically, the UP boys regarded their mothers behavior significantly more often as inconsistent ($t = 1.94$, $p < .05$). The father's behavior was perceived by both groups as similar to that of the mother but the differences were less marked.

A major finding was the consistently lower correlation between mother's and father's perceived behavior in the UP group compared to the AP controls. On Total Score of Positivity (i.e., Positive Interest score minus Hostility score), the correlation between mother's and father's scores differed most ($r = 0.11$ in the UP group versus $r = 0.45$ in the AP group). This finding was apparent in both UP boys and UP girls. It suggests that there is considerably more disagreement between the mother's and the father's parental warmth as perceived by the UP subjects in comparison with the AP controls. UP parents are perceived discordantly, one as warm and the other as cold, which may reflect some kind of compensation mechanism operating in the family.

FOLLOW-UP AT AGES 16-18

Family Relations

In 1979, when the subjects were 16-18 years old, additional questionnaires with a particular focus on family relationships were sent to all the study participants. Analysis of the responses indicates that on *Rohner's* Parental Acceptance-Rejection Self Report Questionnaire (PARQ) the UP boys more frequently rated themselves as being more neglected or rejected by their mothers than by their fathers. The opposite finding was noted among the AP boys. For the UP and AP girls, ratings on the parental acceptance-rejection scale clustered around the mid point; differences between the two groups were not statistically significant. The Czech Child-Marriage-Family Questionnaire indicated that, for the UP subjects, the emotional gap between boys and their mothers widens with the relationship deteriorating over time, whereas the mother-daughter relationship remains stable or improves.

Compared to the AP boys, the UP boys believed that their mothers were less satisfied with them. They described themselves as having more of their fathers' than their mothers' personality characteristics, perceived their parents' marriages as less happy, and considered themselves to be insufficiently informed about sexual matters, especially contraception. Differences between AP and UP girls were negligible in these areas.

Some Conclusions at Age 18

The findings accumulated through adolescence suggest that differences in the development of children born to women twice denied abortion for the same pregnancy and pair-matched controls persist into adolescence. Even if the differences in specific indicators are still not very dramatic and easy to detect at the individual level, they are important in the aggregate, having attained increasing statistical significance over time. The pressure of the particular stresses and frustrations of this developmental period (early to mid-adolescence) seems to act as an aggravating factor, causing even mild psychosocial deviations to become noticeable.

As previously stated, there is in many instances a far-reaching compensation for the originally rejecting attitude of the mother or both parents. In the social integration and competence of UP subjects as a group and in their school achievements, it is the lack of pluses rather than surplus of marked minuses that becomes most apparent. Still, perhaps most important, the fact that differences between UP subjects and AP controls persist and have actually widened after nearly 18 years of family life suggests that "unwantedness" during early pregnancy constitutes a not negligible factor for the child's subsequent life. Socially handicapping characteristics in UP subjects seem to have an accelerating momentum.

FOLLOW-UP AT AGES 21-23

Sample Status

The third follow-up was conducted in 1983-84 when the study participants had become young adults aged 21-23 years. Some were already married and had become parents. Others were in military service or had left Prague. The status of the Prague Cohort and the numbers available for individual interviews are shown in Table 7.1. As noted, 160 UP subjects (74 men and 86 women) and 155 AP controls (70 men and 85 women) were individually examined, a follow-up rate of 73 and 70 percent, respectively.

Table 7.1. Situation at ages 21-23 of the previously "unwanted pregnancy" children (UP) and the control children (AP)

Original number of children in groups N	UP 220	AP 220
Examined so far	160	155
Not yet examined, living in Prague	18	18
In military service	15	25
Moved out of Prague	11	12
Out of the country	4	2
Refused cooperation	7	4
Died	0	2
In custody	4	2
Seriously ill	1	0
	220	220

Data Collection

Current addresses of study participants living in Prague were obtained with the assistance of the Central Population Register. Searches were conducted for relevant independent data stored in other registers, including those maintained by alcoholism and drug treatment centers, the courts, and child-care councils (where diverse contacts with the families of origin had been recorded).

Additional data were obtained through direct follow-up with study participants. Individual structured interviews focused on case histories, present social situation, value orientation, social relations, psychosexual relations, and partner and parent attitudes. Questionnaires and standardized tests elicited information on personality, self-concept, velues, psychosexual and parental attitudes, and related areas. Researchers completed rating scales following interviews and/or home visits. All the methods employed are listed and described in Chapter 10.

The third follow-up was conducted with the same guidelines as before; it consistently adhered to the double blind method, that is, none of the researchers knew which subject belonged to which group. To this day, only the colleague responsible for the original pair-matching knows for certain who is whom.

The follow-up was initiated with two questionnaires sent by mail to all study participants and to their mothers, respectively. The purpose was to obtain basic and current demographic data, inquire about educational experience, and explore psychosexual views and perceptions of family life. Whenever the questionnaires were not returned by a specified date, experienced social workers visited those families, completed the questionnaires separately with the study participants and their mothers, administered other tests, and arranged for a personal interview (which was subsequently confirmed by an invitation addressed to the study participant). Similar personal invitations were dispatched to all participants who returned the mail questionnaire.

Female study participants (both UP and AP) who had married and had children of their own were visited repeatedly. The research focus was extended to include the marital partner and the administration of additional questionnaires designed to assess marital relations and attitudes toward the child. Equal numbers of subjects in both groups had married (50 UP and 50 AP). Eventually, 31 UP couples and 30 AP couples with one child each became available for an exploratory study conducted under double-blind conditions.

An experienced team member (ZD) conducted all the individual structured interviews with study participants at a Marriage Guidance Center located in one of the Prague districts. This procedure assured uniformity of approach and assessment. Subsequently, each participant was asked to take additional tests and complete several questionnaires, as previously described. In all, about two hours were required to finish this segment. Although it was sometimes difficult to confirm appointments, occasionally requiring repeated afforts, cooperation was usually excellent once the subjects had arrived at the Center.

Findings from the Registers

Data from the pupulation registers indicate a greater proneness to social problems among UP study participants than AP controls. For example, as shown in Table 7.2, 57 UP families, compared to 37 AP families, had been registered in the files of the child-care councils. The most frequently indicated reasons were associated with parental divorce, suggesting greater instability in UP families. The files of alcohol and drug treatment centers yielded the names of 10 UP subjects and four AP controls. All were males, except one UP female who was addicted to drugs (Table 7.3).

Table 7.2. Reasons for registration of UP and AP families in Child Care Departments of District National Council in Prague — up to 18 years of age of children

	UP		AP	
	Number	%	Number	%
1. Divorce of parents	21	36.8	13	35.1
2. Intervention in educational and alimony matters	17	29.8	9	24.3
3. Criminal activity of the adolescent	6	10.6	5	13.5
4. Other social and legal reasons	13	22.8	10	27.1
Total	57	100.0	37	100.0

Table 7.3. Apprehension in Alcoholism Treatment Centers in Prague, April—May, 1986 (ages 23-25 years)

	UP	AP
Apprehended once only	1	2
Outpatient treatment	3	1
Compulsory treatment ordered by court, repeated hospitalizations — criminality (usually repeated)	4	0
Drug addiction, plus criminality, repeated hospitalizations	2	1
Total	10	4

Under the category of "drug addiction" in the UP group is one woman — all others on the files of the Alcoholism Treatment Centers are men.

Maladaptation Score Predictions

As explained in the preceding chapter, the Maladaptation Score was developed as a descriptive indicator of maladaptation in psychosocial development and social integration. The higher the score, the more the child be considered as problem-prone and at future risk. Further follow-up in 1985 showed that the average Maladaptation Score at age nine for all UP persons with prison sentences in 1985 was 13.25 (SD 6.94), compared to 10.59 for the total group of UP subjects. Similarly, the average MS at age nine for convicted AP controls was 11.90 (SD 6.41), compared to 8.69 for the total group of AP controls. The differences between those with and without criminal records were statistically highly significant. These differences are even more pronounced when the repeatedly sentenced persons in both groups (MS 15.21; SD 6.16) are compared with first-time offenders (MS 10.80, SD 5.79) and those not registered in the court files (MS 9.33; SD 4.51). The findings confirm the aggregate predictive value of the MS. This observation suggests that the higher average MS among the UP subjects, as compared to the AP controls, reflects an environment that under certain conditions is more likely to foster criminal activity.

Criminal Register

As of 1985, the Criminal Register showed that 41 separate court sentences had been imposed on 23 UP subjects (18 men and five women) compared with 19 individual sentences on 11 AP controls (all men). As shown in Table 7.4, about twice as many UP subjects as AP controls were in the category of offenders receiving the lighter sentences. In the more serious categories, such as custodial sentences and repeated offenses, there were almost three times more UP subjects than AP controls.

The UP group included five women who had already served eight sentences, compared to none among the AP controls.

Table 7.4. Criminal Register data on UP and AP persons, as of November 1985 (ages 22-24 years)

	UP	AP
Number of persons sentenced by court	23	11
men	18	11
women	5	0
Sentenced once	15	8
Sentenced twice	2	2
Sentenced three or more times	6	1
Number of persons sentenced repeatedly	8	3
men	7	3
women	1	0
Total number of sentences imposed	41	19
On probation	15	8
To prison	22	9
Other correctional measures	4	2
Average duration of prison sentence (months)	28	12

Although all the numbers from the alcohol, drug, and criminal registers are small and unsuitable for more sophisticated statistical analysis, the trend is consistently in disfavor of the UP subjects. And there is now an indication, as will also be shown below, that UP girls, who previously seldom differed significantly from AP girls, are experiencing psychological problems similar to those noted earlier only in UP boys.

Follow-Up Data Analysis

Data analysis procedures were similar to those employed in the initial follow-up when the children were around nine years old (see Chapter 6). To assess the statistical significance of differences between the groups, the t-test was used for qualitative data of quantitative nature and chi-square for data derived primarily from qualitative observations. The significance of qualitative differences was verified in two ways. First, the entire UP group (N = 160) was compared with all the AP controls (N = 155), and, second, originally pair-matched UP and AP subjects were compared pair by pair. A total of 112 such pairs were available, allowing a test of significance of differences to be computed by paired chi-square. The second approach could reveal significant differences more sensitively even when chi-square for the whole sample failed to indicate significant differences. However, to avoid ambiguities and reduce chance findings, the comparisons presented here are limited to those where differences were statistically significant as measured both by paired chi-square and the chi-square computed for the entire sample.

Educational Achievement

As noted in Chapter 6, no significant differences were found between the UP subjects and the AP controls on standardized intelligence tests around age nine. Educational attainment by ages 21-23 also did not differ significantly, although it was generally lower for the UP subjects than for the AP controls. For example, more UP than AP subjects acquired only a basic education without serving an apprenticeship (19 % versus 11 %) and, conversely, fewer completed secondary education (42 % of the UP subjects, compared with 56 % of the AP controls). Moreover, the UP mothers were significantly more likely than the AP mothers to express dissatisfaction with the educational level achieved by their children, believing that they could have accomplished more in school.

Life Satisfaction

Perceptions of life satisfaction and social environment were revealed in responses to the first and last questions in the 56-item structured individual interview. The first question asked the study participants to describe their lives thus far and how they would rate them on a given scale. After 54 other questions concerned with diverse aspects of their social environment and their perceptions of their own roles, they were asked to indicate how satisfied they were with their lives at the present time in view of their earlier aspirations and expectations. The distribution of response is shown in Table 7.5.

Table 7.5. Distribution of answers of UP and AP persons to two key questions in the structured interview

At your 20 years, you have had your share of experiences in life. Your life has been so far:	UP %	AP %
1. In accordance with your ideas, generally positive	8.7	31.0
2. Close to your ideas, but there are problems	51.9	51.6
3. Greater problems, worries were prevailing	30.7	15.5
4. "This was not the life I imagined!"	8.7	1.9

$chi^2 = 34.31$, df 3, $p < .001$ (men $p < .001$, women $p < .001$)
chi^2 for matched pairs = 19.51, df = 1, $p < .001$ (men $p < .01$, women $p < .001$)

Finally, tell how you actually feel about your life:		
1. Perfectly satisfied — you can say you are happy	8.1	20.0
2. On the whole satisfied, although there are sometimes problems	55.6	65.8
3. Rather dissatisfied, some life problems worry you a lot	30.0	11.6
4. You are very dissatisfied, cannot cope with your problems	6.2	2.6

$chi^2 = 24.38$, df 3, $p < .001$ (men $p < .001$, women $p < 05$)
chi^2 for matched pairs = 14.78, df = 1, $p < .001$ (men $p < .001$, women $p < .05$)

Less than one third as many UP subjects as AP controls said their lives had developed as expected and more than twice as many stated that they had encountered more problems than anticipated. Only 8 percent of the UP subjects were satisfied with their lives, compared with 20 percent of the AP controls; 36 percent of the UP subjects expressed dissatisfaction, compared with 14 percent of the AP controls. The UP subjects significantly more often than the AP controls attributed their life dissatisfaction to a poor relationship with their parents (paired chi-square $p < .05$). They believed that their parents were dissatisfied with them and let them know it.

Job Satisfaction

There were no significant differences in views expressed by UP subjects and AP controls on how they felt within their present social groups, their concerns about the future, or on how they decided on or prepared for their occupations. Nevertheless, the UP subjects were less satisfied than the AP controls with their present jobs (paired chi-square significant at $p < .02$ for the entire group with males differentiated at $p < .001$ but no significant difference between pair-matched females). Moreover, UP subjects were more dissatisfied with their wages, more often in conflict with their supervisors ($p < .001$), and also less satisfied with their relationships with co-workers ($p < .01$). They also mentioned fewer persons as friends ($p < .001$) and were more often disappointed by them ($p < .001$ for both men and women).

On items related to military service, no significant differences were noted between UP subjects and AP controls. However, significantly fewer of the UP males than the AP controls were promoted to any rank ($p < .01$).

Love Relationships

The UP subjects and AP controls follow an identical pattern as whether, how often, and at what age they were deeply in love, on who first provided information on sexual matters, what circumstances led to their sexual debut, and on their current contraceptive practice (mostly coitus interruptus). There were also no major differences in their opinions on abortion (mostly liberal).

The UP subjects reported repeated disappointments with love relationships more often than the AP controls ($p < .01$) and significantly more of them agreed that "love brings more trouble than pleasure" (paired chi-square $p < .001$ for boys and $p < .01$ for girls). A larger proportion of UP subjects stated that they experienced sexual debut before age 15 with a casual acquaintance ($p < .05$) They also had had many more sexual partners on average (paired chi-square $p < .05$ for UP women and approaching significance for UP boys). The UP males (but not females) significantly more often ($p < .02$) believed that economic considerations are of major importance in marriage and that abortion is an acceptable way of resolving an unwanted pregnancy, entailing limited medical risk. The AP males were less sanguine about abortion and believed it entailed more medical risks.

Views on Breast-Feeding

There were no significant differences between the UP subjects and AP controls regarding their factual knowledge of early child development. It was of interest, however, that the UP subjects, who as young babies had been breast-fed by their mothers for a significantly shorter time than the AP controls, now were more likely to say that a child should be breast-fed for no longer than one month at most.

97

Life Styles

Although individual life style items did not differ between UP subjects and AP controls, it was noted that more UP males and females drank black coffee, that more UP men were heavy smokers, and that UP women drank larger quantities of beer than their AP counterparts did. There was little difference in satisfaction with physical health condition, but more AP women believed that they should lose weight (paired chi-square $p < .02$).

Mental Health

There were marked statistically significant differences in assessments of personal mental health and present mental condition (paired chi-square $p < .001$; women more than men, $p < .01$ and $p < .05$, respectively). UP respondents were more likely to indicate dissatisfaction with their mental well-being, although most felt they still had things under control. However, a significantly greater proportion of UP subjects were actually receiving psychiatric treatment or expressed a need for such therapy ($p < .01$).

Aspiration-Frustration

In the first follow-up, as described in Chapter 6, it was revealed that although there were few significant differences between the UP children and the AP controls on the Aspiration-Frustration Test, the behavior of the UP children, especially boys, was significantly less adaptive in the face of frustration ($p < .05$). The findings were interpreted as suggesting no differences in approaching and solving tasks under normal conditions, but marked differences when working under conditions of even mild stress.

This was borne out more than a decade later when young UP adults proved to be considerably less adaptive than their AP counterparts in a series of real-life situations. Moreover, the observation around age nine of the role of intelligence in coping with frustration was also confirmed in the third follow-up finding that intelligence played less of a role in the adaptation of young adult UP subjects than in the coping behavior of young adult AP controls.

Personal Qualities

The self-administered personality tests, *Eysenck's* (1976) DOPEN and *Spielberger's* (1970) STAI, did not produce any significant differences between the UP subjects and the AP controls taken as a whole. The UP subjects had a higher score for psychoticism and neuroticism on DOPEN than the AP controls but also a lower Lie-score and a higher score for general as well as specific anxiety on STAI, but these did not attain statistical significance. The only statistically significant difference ($p < .02$) was recorded for the UP subjects on extraversion. These differences tended to grow over time among males, while vanishing entirely among females. At ages 21-23, the UP males had a higher score than the AP males on neuroticism ($p < .04$), lower Lie-score ($p < .02$), and revealed more extraversion ($p < .06$). They also had a higher score for anxiety on STAI but the difference was not significant.

Family Relationships

On the *Schludermanns'* CRPBI (Czech standardized version ADOR), the UP young adult males significantly more often rated their mothers as inconsistent ($p < .03$). They also deemed their mothers more hostile and with a less positive interest in them (but these ratings were not statistically significant). There was no difference in the ratings for fathers, just as there were no differences between the groups in the ratings of mothers and fathers by young adult females. In general, these findings corresponded to those noted in the previous follow-up, although less distinctly than at that time. A possible explanation is that when the respondents first completed the questionnaire at age 14-16, they were asked about their current feelings and experiences with parents, whereas in the third follow-up, when they were in their twenties, they were asked to recall how they had felt about their parents at age 14. The same situation applied to *Rohner's* PARQ. Group differences did not reach statistical significance on any of these items althought they were in the expected direction.

Married Participants

The 50 married UP subjects and 50 married AP controls were asked to answer four additional questions, assessing their satisfaction with their marriages and partner relationships. On each item, the differences were statistically more significant for women than for men, which suggests, that UP women perceived themselves as experiencing less satisfactory marital relationships than the UP men did. However, on three of the four items the responses differed significantly between the groups of UP subjects and AP controls. The young UP adults, born to women twice denied abortion for the same pregnancy, judged their own marriages as less happy than the married AP controls ($p < .01$). If they could start all over again, the UP subjects would significantly more often prefer not to marry or not to marry their present partner ($p < .01$). However, they also admitted significantly more often than the AP controls that they might be to blame for the present situation, that they did not do enough to make the marriage work, or that they behaved in ways that could result in marital breakup ($p < .01$). Below the level of significance for the group of UP subjects, but above it for UP women ($< .05$), was the perception that the partner also did not do all that was necessary for the marriage to succeed.

UP and AP Parents

Special attention was paid to the 34 couples in both groups who had a child. The research workers were able to visit and complete extensive examinations with 31 families in which either husband or wife was originally a UP child and with 30 families in which one parent had been a AP control. (At the time, there were nine UP fathers and 22 UP mothers, along with six AP fathers and 24 AP mothers). The sample size was too small for statistical analysis but the observations noted to date will form the basis for the next stage of this longitudinal study, which will focus on "children of unwanted children."

Interviews with the young UP mothers suggested that, compared to the AP control mothers, their pregnancies were less often welcome. They were less well prepared for accepting maternity and required more time to develop a close relationship with the developing fetus. Most of the UP mothers planned to stay home until the child was two years old, that is, until the end of their paid maternity leave, while most of the AP mothers expected to stay home with the child until it reached school age. Grandmothers were reported to be providing greater assistance in young families where one partner was a former UP child, but it is not known as yet whether that grandmother was the one whose original request for abortion was denied or the mother of the UP child's partner.

Another difference between the young UP and AP families showed up in the mother's major sources of information about pregnancy, delivery, and early child development. The UP mothers listed their physicians as the primary source, followed by the media, and their mothers a distant third. The young AP mothers listed their own mothers first, with other sources of information far behind.

Researchers who conducted double-blind evaluations of the families rated the UP mothers as stricter and less able to "feel with the child," but no less warm or careful than the AP mothers. The fathers married to the UP women were, however, deemed to be markedly less warm, less careful with the child, and less oriented to the family than were the fathers of children born to AP control women. However, these are only preliminary observations based on a very small sample.

Psychosocial Instability Score (PSIS)

A Psychosocial Instability Score was constructed on the basis of structured interview responses to 37 items which, based on clinical experience, were considered indicative of unsatisfactory or problematic relationships within the personal sphere or the psychosocial environment. It is an ad hoc measure similar to the previously de-scribed Maladaptation Score (see Chapter 6). The 37 items are divided into six sub-scales, assessing self-concept and life satisfaction, original family environment and family relations, attitudes toward occupation and job environment, satisfaction with love relationships, relations with friends and acquaintances, and knowledge of early child development and care. Subscores were developed by calculating the number of negative responses in each subscale, and then adding the total into a single Psy-chosocial Instability Score for each UP subject and AP control.

Since the number of items in the separate subscales differs, only the difference in scores between the groups is presented in Table 7.6. To facilitate comparisons, dif-

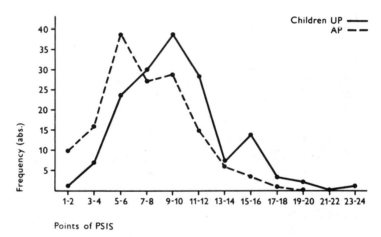

Fig. 7.1. Psychosocial Instability Score (PSIS) (all examined UP and AP subjects).

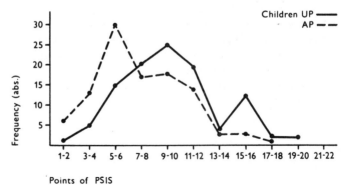

Fig. 7.2. Psychosocial Instability Score (PSIS) (paired UP and AP subjects).

101

ferences between the groups and the Maladaptation Score around age nine are also shown. It is apparent that the differences in what the study participants said about themselves at ages 21-23 tend to be even greater than the differences in what parents, teachers, and schoolmates said about them more than a decade earlier. However, the gap noted between UP boys and girls at about age nine appears to have greatly diminished as they reached young adulthood.

Table 7.6. Differences in psychosocial Instability Scores of young UP and AP adults

Scales of Psychosocial Instability	Total Sample		Young Men		Young Women	
	UP N = 159	AP 150	UP 73	AP 66	UP 86	AP 84
	t-test	p	t-test	p	t-test	p
1. Personal well-being	2.87	< .01	2.96	< .01	1.49	n.s.
2. Relation to the original family	3.21	< .01	2.98	< .01	1.88	< .05
3. Relation to occupation	1.98	< .05	2.01	< .01	0.72	n.s.
4. Erotic and sexual relations	4.31	< .001	3.12	< .002	3.02	< .01
5. Relations to friends and mates	1.00	n.s.	0.35	n.s.	1.19	n.s.
6. Knowledge of child development	0.97	n.s.	1.05	n.s.	0.44	n.s.
Total score of psychosocial instability	5.50	< .001	4.69	< .001	3.10	< .002
Differences in original Maladaptation Scores of these persons UP N = 159, AP N = 150	3.90	< .001	3.14	< .002	2.61	< .01

Concluding Note

Many questions have been raised over the years about specific aspects and the implications of the longitudinal study of the Prague Cohort. To the extent possible, they are discussed in Chapter 9. Suffice it to say here that the 1983-84 follow-up of the children born in 1961-63 to Prague women twice denied abortion for the same pregnancy and their pair-matched controls provides further evidence that, in the aggregate, unwanted pregnancies entail an increased risk for the subsequent development of the child. Differences between these children and those born following accepted pregnancies have continued to widen over time, influencing quality of life in adolescence and young adulthood, and perhaps even casting a shadow on the next generation.

Chapter 8

The Northern Finland Cohort, 1966-82
A Follow-Up Study of Children Unwanted at Birth

Antero Myhrman

Editors' Note

The Northern Finland studies of children unwanted by their mothers during the late stages of gestation were initiated in 1966 by Dr. *Paula Rantakallio,* Professor in the Department of Public Health Science, University of Oulu. Dr. *Rantakallio* has encouraged subsequent follow-up efforts, including pair-matched control studies conducted by *Antero Myhrman,* a colleague in the Department of Public Health Science. The Finnish investigators organized the First International Workshop on Longitudinal Studies of Unwanted Children, convened in Oulu in June 1985. Additional reports were presented at that time by Dr. *Harriet Forsius,* Associate Professor of Child Psychiatry, and by *Leila Seitamo,* Chief Psychologist in the Department of Pediatrics, University of Oulu. From the beginning, the Northern Finland studies were encouraged by Dr. *Ole Wasz-Höckert,* Professor of Pediatrics, University of Helsinki, and by the Sigrid Juselius Foundation. The following chapter is based on material originally prepared by *Antero Myhrman,* building on his efforts and those of his colleagues.

Background

The Northern Finland study of unwanted children is based on a cohort of 12,058 children born in 1966 to 11,931 women residing in the two northernmost provinces of Finland (Oulu and Lapland). The inquiry was initiated in the prenatal clinics during the 24th to 28th week of pregnancy and covered 96 percent of all deliveries in the region (*Rantakallio,* 1969, 1974, 1985). Midwives used questionnaires to obtain demographic, biological, and socioeconomic background information on each woman and her family. They also noted the psychological condition of the women and asked about the desirability of their present pregnancy. Of the 11,737 women who responded, 63 percent stated that the pregnancy "occurred at a propitious time" (Accepted Pregnancy/AP); 25 percent indicated their pregnancy "would have been more desirable later" (Later Pregnancy/LP); and 12 percent said that it "should not have occurred at all" (Unwanted Pregnancy/UP). Only 194 women (1.6 %) refused to respond to this question. Analysis of the questionnaires showed that the UP women tended to be older than the AP and LP women, more often unmarried, widowed or divorced, had more children, and lived under poorer socioeconomic conditions in more remote villages.

Follow-up studies of the entire cohort were conducted at 28 days after birth and in 1980-81 when the children were 14-15 years old (*Rantakallio*, 1985). Pair-matched control studies were initiated at age eight and repeated at age 16. A sample of the UP children was matched with AP children in terms of age, sex, birth order, number of siblings, mother's age and marital status, place of residence, and social group according to father's occupation at the time of the child's birth and later (*Rantakallio* and *Myhrman*, 1980; *Myhrman*, 1982, 1985; *Myhrman, Seitamo* and *Forsius*, 1984). This chapter describes the organization and evolution of the study, the several samples, and major findings in chronological order. Discussions with Prague colleagues were of material assistance in the second follow-up.

The 1966 Cohort

The sample consists of 11,931 mothers who delivered 11,744 individual infants and 314 twins in 1966. The cohort includes 96 percent of all births occurring in Northern Finland at the time. Analysis of the questionnaires completed at 24-26 weeks of pregnancy showed that the UP mothers who did not want that pregnancy were considerably older (32.6 years) than either the AP mothers who wanted the pregnancy (28.1 years) or the LP mothers who would have preferred the pregnancy at a later date (26.6 years). These differences were statistically highly significant. The mean number of children (including the expected child) was more than twice as high for the UP women (5.2) than for the AP women (2.5) and also significantly higher than for the LP women (2.8), who were younger than the AP women. The percentage of mothers already having four or more children was 55.4 precent among UP women, 16.1 percent among LP women, and 12.2 percent among AP women. The percentage of wanted pregnancies decreased with increasing parity.

Of the AP women, 99 percent were married, compared to 96.2 percent of the LP women and 81.1 percent of the UP women. Widowed or divorced women were included with the unmarrieds because of their small number. The mean age at marriage of the AP mothers (22.4 years) was similar to that of the UP mothers (22.4 years, whereas the LP mothers tended to be younger at marriage (21.6 years). The mean interval between marriage and the present birth corresponded roughly to mean ages (11.2 years for UP mothers, 5.3 years for AP mothers, and 4.6 years for LP mothers). The mean interval between pregnancies was 2.4 years for UP mothers, 1.9 years for LP mothers, and 3.0 years for AP mothers. All the differences between AP mothers and the LP and UP mothers were statistically highly significant.

The percentage of premarital conceptions was studied among the married women expecting their first child. A conception was considered premarital if the time between marriage and expected date of delivery was shorter than 252 days, that is, more than one menstrual period shorter than the duration of normal pregnancy calculated from the first day of the last menstrual bleeding. The percentage was highest among the UP mothers (91.7 %), followed by the LP mothers (77.2 %), and the AP mothers (31.4 %).

Statistically significant differences were also noted in place of residence. AP mothers tended to live more often in towns (36.2 %), whereas UP mothers resided most often in remote villages (58.3 %) and LP mothers fell in between. Highly significant differences were noted in distances to the nearest prenatal clinic, with the longest for UP women and the shortest for AP women.

Social status, as determined by the father's occupation, consisted of four categories, with a fifth category for farmers (whose status was determined by the size of their land holdings). Social status was highest in the AP group (7.9 % in Class 1, compared to 2.2 % for the UP group and 4.2 % for the LP group). The lowest category of poor farmers included 30.5 percent of the UP group, compared to 13.1 percent of the AP group and 12.8 percent of the LP group. The percentage of managers and officials was significantly higher in the AP group (19.5 %) than in the LP group (11.6 %) or the UP group (6.8 %). The UP mothers had had the least amount of schooling, with 26.8 percent having less than five years of primary school, compared to 6.5 percent of the AP mothers and 5.1 percent of the LP mothers. Only 4.9 percent of the UP women had had at least five years' secondary schooling, compared to 13.3 precent of the AP women and 10.0 percent of the LP women. The percentage of mothers not working outside the home was highest among the UP women (79.8 %), compared to the AP and LP women (57.5 % for both). However, a significantly larger proportion of the UP women, many of whom worked on farms, described their daily tasks as very strenuous or strenuous (30.3 %), compared to the AP women (12.5 %) and LP women (16.1 %). In remote areas of the region particularly, agriculture constitutes the main sector of the economy. The general standard of living is lower and educational opportunities are fewer.

The midwives conducting the prenatal survey had also been instructed to observe the women's "frame of mind" when asking them to classify the wantedness of their present pregnancy. Of the UP women, 33 percent were rated as depressed and 17.6 percent as very depressed, compared to 4.6 percent and 0.6 percent among the AP women and 16.0 percent and 1.7 percent among the LP women. In other words, 94.8 percent of the AP women were deemed normal, compared to 82.3 percent of the LP women and only 49.4 percent of the UP women. These differences were statistically highly significant.

At the time the study was initiated in 1965-66, there was little public discussion in Finland of contraception or abortion. From 1951 until 1970, it was possible to obtain a legal abortion only on well-defined medical grounds when authorized by two physicians. Social factors could be taken into considerations an additional indication. Around 1965, there were about 5,000 abortions and 80,000 births annually in Finland, indicating an abortion ratio of 62 per 1,000 live births (*Järvinen*, 1971). There was no organized family planning program and health services were limited. Only seven obstetricians served the total population of 600,000 people in Northern Finland. Women living in the more remote areas were often poorer, had less education, and had longer distances to travel to obtain contraceptive advice or services than those living in towns. While family planning was not officially discouraged, neither was it encouraged. The women who indicated during the late stage of pregnancy that their pregnancy should not have occurred at all expressed an attitude that may be classified as "unwanted." They did not, however, apply for abortion, in part because they must have known that their situation did not meet the eligibility requirements stipulated by the then prevailing legislation.

The 1970 abortion legislation permits termination on request if the woman has already given birth to four children. Some 55 percent of the UP women would have qualified for this provision had the more liberal abortion legislation been in effect five years earlier. Most of the primiparous women with unwanted pregnancies were unmarried and nearly all of the others in this group conceived premaritally. Under the 1970 abortion legislation, unmarried status alone would have been an acceptable indication for legal termination.

In sum, it was concluded that the unwanted pregnancies had occurred partly as the result of inefficient family planning practices and inadequate family planning services, interacting with complex multidimensional personal and social factors.

Follow-Up at 28 Days

The course of the perinatal period was least favorable for the children born from UP pregnancies. Their weight and length at birth were smaller. The proportion of children with birth weight below 2,500 grams was 3.7 percent in the AP group, 4.4 percent in the LP group, and 5.2 percent in the UP group, the difference between the AP and UP groups being statistically significant. The proportion born prematurely (less than 38 weeks gestation) was 7.8 percent in the AP group, 10.4 percent in the LP group, and 11.7 percent in the UP group, the difference between the AP and UP groups again being statistically significant. There was no statistically significant difference in perinatal mortality or the percentage of children treated in children's hospitals. Overall, there was no clear indication that unwantedness had caused deleterious physical effects on UP children during the perinatal period. The differences noted could have stemmed from the less favorable social, economic, and biological conditions prevailing among the UP mothers.

Follow-Up at Age Eight

In 1974, when the children were eight years old and had completed their first year of school (which begins at age seven in Finland), a pair-matched study was initiated. Some 300 UP children, about 20 percent of the total number of children born from unwanted pregnancies, were selected by systematic sampling based on the serial numbers printed on the original questionnaires used by the midwives during the prenatal interviews. This procedure ensured representation of the diverse geographic and population sectors within the region, as well as seasons of birth. Each UP child thus selected was matched with an AP control child, born to a woman who had considered her pregnancy propitious at the time. The matching proceeded on the basis of the mother's marital status and parity, social grouping according to the father's occupation, and place of residence in terms of population density. Most of the women who had been unmarried during the original prenatal survey had married by the time the child was eight years old. However, between 1967 and 1974, and additional 111 children were born to UP women and 178 children to AP women, a statistically significant difference (*Myhrman*, 1982).

Questionnaires were sent separately to each family and every child's teacher, with a request to participate in a survey of child health. No mention was made of the basis for selecting these children. Responses were received from 95 percent of the parents and 90 percent of the teachers. The main topics in the family questionnaire were social well-being and family constellation, while the teacher's questionnaires focused on the child's biological, social, and educational development.

Data became available for 147 UP boys and 138 AP boys, and for 133 UP girls and 141 AP girls. No significant differences were noted between UP and AP boys or girls in mean body weight or height or hospital admissions. In the aggregate, girls achieved better school grades than boys. While differences in school performance between UP and AP children did not reach levels of statistical significance, differences noted were consistently to the disadvantage of the UP children. For example, they required considerably more special teaching attention to master difficulties in learning reading and writing skills, as well as in other theoretically grounded subjects. Their verbal performance, as assessed by teachers, was significantly poorer (*Myhrman*, 1982). No differences between the UP and AP children were observed in emotional development or in the frequency with which they played with friends at home or participated in different types of children's clubs. The UP children had slightly less equipment for sports and hobbies, and less often had the company of their parents after school hours (*Rantakallio*, 1985).

Upward and downward social mobility was measured by social status according to the father's occupation at the time of the child's birth and eight years later. There was significantly more downward mobility and less upward mobility among the families of the UP children, compared to the AP children. Some 10 percent of the UP families had emigrated to Sweden, compared to 4 percent of the AP families (*Myhrman*, 1977). On the whole, the follow-up study at age eight showed slightly poorer development among the UP children, which could be ascribed to unwantedness in late pregnancy or to differences in family social conditions, or to a combination of these factors.

107

Follow-Up at Age 14

A follow-up of the entire cohort was conducted in 1980-81 when the children were 14 years old. Of the original 12,058 children, 278 had died, leaving 11,780 for. follow-up. Of these 11,780 children, 82.9 percent resided in Northern Finland, 10.7 percent had moved elsewhere in Finland, and 6.4 percent had emigrated with their families to other countries, mainly Sweden. The good results achieved in tracing the children were due primarily to the reliable population registration system and national registers. However, tracking the last 10 percent required more time and effort than the remaining 90 percent together. Data thus became available on all the children, except the 14 who had emigrated.

Once the addresses of the families were known, a questionnaire concerning the child's school performance and health and the family's social status was mailed to each of the children and their families. If no answer was received, a repeat request was sent. Eventually replies were obtained from 97 percent of the families. For the remaining 3 percent, inquiries were made of school nurses concerning the child's health and of the school principals concerning school performance. Doubtful responses returned by families were also checked in this way. Children known to be mentally retarded, or living in severely incapacitating circumstances, were not included in the survey. In all, the research team had access to the population register, the death register, the hospital discharge register, the medical reimbursement register, the child subsistence for ill children register, and the register of mentally retarded children.

Review of the findings showed a higher rate of infant mortality among the UP children (24 deaths per 1,000 births) compared to the AP children (14.2 per 1,000), a difference that was statistically very significant. The UP children had higher incidences of all types of handicaps, the differences with AP children being statistically highly significant for cerebral palsy and mental retardation. The proportion of IQ level below 86 was 52 per 1,000 among the UP children versus 20 per 1,000 among the AP children. Physical growth was also poorer among the UP children; their mean height at age 14 was 1.4 cm less among the UP boys, compared to AP boys, and 1 cm less among UP girls, compared to AP girls. School performance was significantly lower among the UP children when compared to the AP children, but the sex difference was still wider, with UP girls outperforming AP boys (*Rantakallio*, 1985).

Follow-Up at Age 16

A second pair-matched follow-up study was conducted in 1982 when most of the children were in their last year of compulsory public school at age 16. A series of 88 UP children (41 boys and 47 girls) and 89 AP children (43 boys and 46 girls) were matched for sex and number of children in the family, mother's age, marital

108

status, and parity; and mother's social status based on 1966 and 1980 data so as to reduce the possible influence of upward and downward social mobility and changes in marital status (*Myhrman, Seitamo,* and *Forsius,* 1984; *Myhrman,* 1985). Some 33.3 percent of UP boys and 34.6 percent of AP boys and 43.5 percent of UP girls and 44.6 percent of AP girls responded to invitations for personal interviews. No statistically significant differences were noted on the matched variables between respondents and nonrespondents. All interviews were individually conducted by the same researcher (AM). The questionnaire items, psychological tests, and interviews with teachers were all modeled on the experience of the Prague colleagues (see Chapters 6 and 7). The approach was designed to focus attention on each child's perceptions of his/her childhood and family relations, attitudes toward school, and future adulthood. Teachers were requested to complete a questionnaire about every child's behavior and school achievement.

While the boys continued to be poorer school achievers than the girls, some significant differences were apparent. The performance of UP and AP boys was about the same. However, the school grades of UP girls had declined below those of AP girls, with a significant difference in the grade for school performance. The teachers' ratings for character and ability were similarly unfavorable for the UP girls, as were their relations with the teachers and fellow classmates and assessment for tidiness in comparison to the AP girls. More UP girls were reluctant to go to school (27.7 %) than were AP girls (8.7 %), a difference that is statistically significant. UP girls more frequently wanted to leave school at the earliest possible age, a choice supported by their parents who, more often than AP parents, expressed the view that compulsory school was enough and that there was little purpose in school continuation (*Myhrman, Seitamo,* and *Forsius,* 1984).

Assessment of parent-child relations indicated perceptions that UP and AP mothers had devoted about equal effort to childrearing. However, UP girls believed their fathers had been more distant; 45.5 percent expressed the view that their fathers had participated less in their upbringing than was usually the case in average families. Only 19.6 percent of the AP girls expressed this opinion, a statistically significant difference. No such difference was found among the boys. Traumatic experiences in upbringing were mentioned by 27.6 percent of the UP girls, compared to 8.7 percent of the AP controls, another statistically significant difference not noted among the boys (*Myhrman, Seitamo,* and *Forsius,* 1984).

The Children's Report of Parental Behavior Inventory also reflected difficulties in father-daughter relationships. UP girls perceived their fathers to be less positively interested, more hostile, and more inconsistent in their behavior, with the differences with AP girls' perceptions of their fathers being statistically significant in all three areas. UP boys perceived their fathers more positively than did AP boys; the difference on autonomy reached statistical significance. No differences were noted in perceptions of the mothers by UP or AP boys or girls. Some of these findings may be reflections of traditional attitudes toward boys and girls in Northern Finland.

109

Conclusions

It will be recalled that in the original prenatal assessment of the Northern Finland sample unwantedness of the pregnancy was closely associated with poor socioeconomic conditions and future uncertainties. In the subsequent eight years, these women and their families experienced more downward mobility than did the AP and LP women. Moreover, fewer of the unmarried UP mothers entered into marriage. Infant mortality was higher and handicaps were overrepresented in the UP mothers group, but no differences were found on other health indicators.

School performance was poorer among the UP children, but no significant differences were noted in the pair-matched studies. Whereas UP boys had more problems than AP boys in earlier school years, this situation was reversed in later years when UP girls had more difficulties than AP girls. Although more than half the UP mothers had experienced emotional distress about the unwanted pregnancy, they were apparently able to cope. Difficulties in parent-child relationships were found more often between UP fathers and UP daughters than between UP or AP mothers and either sons or daughters or AP fathers and AP daughters. The findings suggest that in Northern Finland one of the consequences of unwantedness during pregnancy is paternal rather than maternal deprivation.

On the whole, the Northern Finland studies indicate that unwantedness during pregnancy was frequently associated with less favorable socioeconomic conditions, a combination leading to subsequent developmental problems with more unfavorable consequences for girls than for boys. Most of the women who frankly stated in 1966 that their pregnancy "should not have occurred at all" would have been eligible for abortion on request, meeting the conditions of the abortion legislation promulgated in 1970, had they wanted it. The prevention of unwanted pregnancy is more important than ever for the well-being of the family.

Chapter 9

Questions and Answers: Discussion and Suggestions

Zdeněk Matějček, Henry P. David, Zdeněk Dytrych, and Vratislav Schüller

Segments of the research reported in this monograph have been previously published and discussed in national and international seminars and conferences over the past 20 or more years. The Prague Cohort study in particular has attracted considerable attention, often focused on its pair-matched methodology or on specific findings. This chapter summarizes the major questions that have been raised and provides some answers. Topics covered include the possible influences of organic damage during pregnancy, heredity, prenatal conditions, siblings, and divorces and remarriages, plus effects on abortion policy and whether or not the UP children knew they were born from unwanted pregnancies.

Comparisons are also made between findings from the Prague Cohort study and the related but not identical studies in Sweden and Northern Finland. The chapter ends with some concluding observations and suggestions for further research and educational policies designed to reduce the incidence of unwanted pregnancies.

Organic Damage

One of the most frequent questions has been whether the deviations noted in the development of the UP children might have resulted from possible organic damage to the fetus during pregnancy rather than psychosocial influences after birth. Some colleagues who ask this question refer to symptoms of minimal brain dysfunction or the behavior of children born of alcohol-dependent mothers.

Our response is that the case histories of both the UP children and the AP controls were reviewed in great detail with the parents. Circumstances that could have led to prenatal brain damage or dysfunction (including maternal alcohol and/or drug abuse) were found to be about the same in both groups. Compared to the AP children, the UP children did not show more signs of major biological stress during their intrauterine life.

It had been hypothesized in the initial follow-up that more sings of minimal brain damage would be found among the UP children than among the AP controls. However, thorough examination at age nine by an experienced neurologist/pediatrician (who did not know which child belonged to which group) failed to support the hypothesis. The incidence of signs of minimal brain damage was about the same in both groups.

An important finding did emerge from further analysis of the first follow-up data. A Maladaptation Score one standard deviation higher than for the total group of UP children was found in two thirds of the UP children with minimal brain damage, while only one third of the AP controls with minimal brain dysfunction had a Maladaptation Score one standard deviation higher than that of the total group of AP controls.

Despite similar organic findings and the same deviations in nervous system function, there were many more UP children than AP controls whose nonadaptive behavior in the family, at school, and in the peer group differed strikingly from that of other children. This finding suggests that some of the UP children have "something in excess" which then combines with the basic biological impairment but is not operative in the similarly biologically damaged AP controls. This "something in excess" may be attributed to the emotional atmosphere, family interaction, developmental stimulation, social learning, and all other factors related to the family context. While our findings do not preclude the possibility of adverse prenatal influences, they provide stronger evidence for a hypothesis emphasizing the importance and influence of parental attitudes adopted during the child's postnatal development.

Heredity

When the question of hereditary influences is raised, the reference is usually to personality features that can be transmitted by hereditary mechanisms. From this perspective, many mothers of the UP children constitute a heredity-conditioned sample that is less socially competent, as evidenced by their failure to obtain a legal or illegal abortion when other women in similar circumstances were able to do so. Moreover, they are inadequate in developing satisfactory social contacts, at first resenting the unwanted pregnancy but often coming to terms relatively easily with the resulting child. Although difficult to define, these women are considered distinct personalities, with their children taking after them. And for some colleagues that may explain why the UP children differ from the AP controls.

Heredity was investigated in the case histories of all the Prague Cohort study participants. As shown in Table 6.16 (see page 72), there were no differences between the UP children and the AP controls on heredity-conditioned psychological or somatic pathology. Of course, the proposition that the UP mothers constitute a special population sample cannot be entirely refuted. It may well be that an unwanted pregnancy is in itself a "selective" factor. If there are other selective factors, such as a twice repeated application for abortion, insufficient reasons for applying, or an application submitted too late, etc., the selection is even more marked. In 1961-63 only 2 percent of all abortion applications were rejected on second request by the Prague Abortion Appeals Commission. There is thus a definite selection factor — one that seems well suited for the study of unwanted children.

However, the mothers of the UP children are not a homogeneous group, as indicated in the discussion of the continuum of wantedness (see page 31). They differed in their attitudes toward the pregnancy and the child's birth and also in their retrospective report regarding the original abortion application; 38 percent of these women denied on direct questioning that they had ever requested an abortion for this pregnancy. To our surprise, standard personality tests revealed no marked differences between the UP and AP mothers. Two psychiatrists conducting individual interviews were unable to differentiate between these women. However, clear differences were noted by visiting social workers and by teachers who knew the families through the children and became aware of the atmosphere these women had created for their children's development.

We suggest that, while some "selection-based" factor may have been at play in the group of UP women, whatever differences existed between them and the AP women were slight and socially inconspicuous. This was in marked contrast to the sizable differences between the children. For example, the Maladaptation Score distinguished between the two groups of women but at a level of statistical significance far lower than the highly significant difference between the UP children and the AP controls. Moreover, the clinical picture of subdeprivation presented by the UP children implies that more factors are involved than a genetic transfer of personality traits from mothers to children, although some degree of impact cannot be ruled out. Again, it appears that the psychosocial development of the UP children includes "something in excess" which cannot be explained solely by hereditary transfer. Moreover, considering the highly heterogeneous input from the fathers and the possible polygenetic transfer of traits, it is even less likely that the differences in development between the UP children and AP controls resulted entirely from hereditary factors.

Regression analysis showed a significant relationship between the mother's and her child's Maladaptation Scores. This is in accordance with the expectation that the more problematic the mother's personality and life situation, the greater the developmental risk to which the child will be exposed. However, this relationship applied to both the UP and the AP group, and was even stronger and more significant in the AP than in the UP group. If in these circumstances the UP children and the AP controls differ so significantly on the Maladaptation Score, it appears that this cannot be attributed solely to maternal maladaptation, whether due to heredity or to external life conditions and circumstances. It seems rather more likely that "something in excess" is operative in the family context of the UP children and may be more decisive in its impact than possible hereditary factors.

Prenatal Influences

Another set of questions comes from the field of prenatal psychology. On the basis of their experience with psychotherapy and hypnosis with individual patients, specialists in prenatal psychology have constructed a hypothesis about a close, and sometimes even fatal, link between a woman's attitude toward her pregnancy and the later formation of her child's personality.

There is a basic assumption that the growing fetus "perceives" the mother's emotions and enters into psychological interaction with her well before its nervous system has developed very substantially. Another assumption holds that what has been psychologically encoded in the earliest stages of the child's development, that is, during embryonic and fetal development, has stronger and more lasting effects than later events in the postnatal period.

In discussions of the Prague Cohort, specialists in prenatal psychology are often disappointed that the findings are not more unfavorable for the UP subjects. For example, the UP group recorded no more malformations, premature births, stillborn babies, or cases of mental retardation than the AP controls. Moreover, there were no substantial differences in physical or intellectual development. The existing deviations were slight, but they were nevertheless real and socially distressing.

In discussing the experience of specialists in prenatal psychology it becomes apparent that many of their observations are based on a small number of individual case studies and employ retrospective reports derived from hypnosis and reconstructions evolving from the psychotherapeutic process. This is rather different from the prospective longitudinal approach of the Prague Cohort study and its comparatively large sample, which may be more representative of society and its sociocultural context at a given moment in time than the patients who present themselves in clinical practice and actively seek therapeutic services.

Some prenatal psychologists note that the UP group includes mothers who can be said to have selected themselves by consciously rejecting their pregnancy. In twice confronting the abortion commissions these women are thought to have demonstrated a strong ego structure. This circumstance is far more favorable than a subconscious rejection of the pregnancy, which would mean that a woman would not outwardly manifest her negative attitude and would not have been selected for participation in the study. And a major aim of the project was to show the interconnection between the UP child's psychosocial development and the conscious and outwardly manifested attitudes of the parents, as compared to AP controls.

In attributing the postnatal problems associated with "unwantedness" to prenatal experience of the developing embryo or fetus, there appears to be a certain "glossing over" of previous studies of mother/child interaction and of psychological deprivation seen in children in substitute family care. The Prague findings are more in concert with these earlier studies, suggesting that parental attitudes become operational only when both parents (the father as well as the mother) perceive their child as an independent being that has actively entered their world, makes demands on them, interacts with them, and responds to the social environment in a complex and creative manner.

It may well be correct that prenatal influences can have a substantial impact on the postnatal behavior and development of certain individuals. That does not, however, negate the importance of postnatal influences. It will be recalled that many of the UP children demonstrated healthy personalities and developed more in accord with established standard criteria than some of the AP controls. This observation suggests the existence of compensatory mechanisms, which could counteract the effects of unfavorable prenatal conditioning.

Siblings

In discussion of the Czech, Finnish, and Swedish studies, questions are often asked about the siblings of the UP children and whether they were included in the observations. Of the 220 UP children in Prague, there were 50 only children, 54 had only younger siblings, and 116 had only older siblings. We agree that the siblings might have provided a kind of validity test. If they proved to exhibit the same kind of deviations from the norm as the studied UP children, such findings could not be interpreted as having a direct relationship to the unwanted pregnancy. More consideration would have to be given to heredity, parents' personalities, or other relatively constant factors.

While it was not possible to examine the siblings to the same extent as the UP children and the AP controls, the case histories obtained from the parents included several questions regarding siblings' health, school achievement, and behavior problems (if any). The siblings of the UP children and of the AP controls did not differ significantly on any of the observed variables. Even if they had, it would have been very difficult to interpret the findings. The position of each child in the family differs, with age, sex, and parity presenting a bewildering maze of combinations that is well nigh impossible to control.

In the Prague Cohort, a very important subgroup consists of only children whose family situation is uncomplicated by siblings. As noted, the UP onlies have the highest (worst) Maladaptation Score, while the AP onlies have the lowest (best). Moreover, regression analysis of maladaptation scores showed that neither the UP children nor the AP controls appeared as better or worse when considered in terms of number of siblings (see Table 6.24, page 82). At the same time, the groups did differ significantly, depending on whether they were perceived positively or negatively by their families.

As they grow older, the UP children and AP controls, now young adults, will further confront the realities of life. Present plans for the next follow-up include the collection of hard, independent data from available registers for both the study participants and their siblings.

Divorces and Remarriages

The question has been asked whether the differences found between the UP subjects and the AP controls might be due to the more frequent divorce in the families of the UP children after they were born rather than the unwantedness at the beginning of their lives. The available evidence suggests otherwise. The absolute number of divorces is not very high (29 in the UP and 18 in the AP group). Moreover, the average Maladaptation Score (MS) of UP children whose parents divorced is not significantly different from the average of the total sample of the UP children (MS = 10.71, SD 5.73 versus MS = 10.59, SD 5.35). Although the average MS of AP children whose parents divorced (MS = 9.92) is higher than the average of the total sample of AP children (MS = 8.69), the difference is not statistically significant. The finding is similar for UP children who appear in the child-care council files with a reference to "education and alimony adjustments"; the MS of these UP children is not significantly different from the MS of UP children not registered in the files. Since the differences between the maladaptation scores of UP children and AP controls are statistically highly significant, it can only be concluded that the maladaptation tendency of the UP children existed before the divorce and that it was as intense as that of the UP children whose family structure was not disrupted by divorce.

There is some evidence from regression analysis that the presence of a stepfather has different effects in the UP group than in the AP control group (see Table 6.24, page 82). However, as noted, external unsettling events, such as divorce and remarriage, in the lives of the UP mothers do not explain the differences between the Maladaptation Scores of their children and those of the children of AP control mothers (exposed to similar family instability).

Effects on Abortion Policy

Colleagues from abroad have often inquired whether the Government of Czechoslovakia, which provided major support for the Prague studies, showed an interest in the findings and their implications for abortion legislation. Czechoslovak laws have long expressed empathy with women distressed by unwanted pregnancy. As noted in Chapter 6, since 1957 a woman has not been held criminally liable if she performed an abortion on herself or if she consented to pregnancy termination for nonmedical reasons. However, women have had to appear before abortion commissions to request termination of unwanted pregnancies for reasons consonant with prevailing legislation, however interpreted. This requirement was imposed even in those instances where women had a clear statutory right to abortion on request. Rarely was consideration given to a woman's psychological maturity, her psychosocial readiness to accept a maternal role, or willingness to assume child-caring responsibilities alone or with the natural father.

The extensive interviews with the UP women who acknowledged having requested an abortion revealed that the vast majority experienced ambivalence on discovering their pregnancy. They engaged in a complicated decision-making process, considering positive and negative implications of continuing the pregnancy. This involved not only the woman's own life situation but also her perceptions of the views of important others, including her partner, parents, family members, and sometimes even very close friends, plus the influences exerted by career prospects, employer attitudes, etc. Contradictory advice intensified the ambivalence and inner conflicts up to the time of consulting with the gynecologist and the official confirmation of the reality of her pregnancy. If at this point the woman decided to request pregnancy termination, her own decision-making became subject to the concurrence of the district abortion commission, or, eventually, the regional appellate commission.

The UP women willing to talk about their experience with the abortion commission expressed a wide range of attitudes. They varied from quite positive (the commission's refusal to grant the request was correct and the woman was grateful to have a happy and healthy child), to quite negative (the commission's refusal was tragic and cast a cloud on the woman's subsequent fate and the child's development). The overwhelming majority did not consider the commission's function as personally helpful but rather as a psychologically insensitive "official interference" with a private decision-making process. (It should be noted that the researchers who interviewed those women never saw them again and were thus able to preserve the anonymity and confidentiality of the study.)

The findings from the Prague studies contributed to a gradual reconsideration of the prevailing abortion legislation. Following considerable public debate and media discussion, the Czech and Slovak National Councils enacted identically revised statutes, which were implemented as of 1 January 1987 (Codex No. 66/1986). They emphasize the need for preventing unwanted pregnancies by education for planned and responsible parenthood in the family, at school, and through health organizations; order that medical examinations and contraceptives available only on prescription be provided free of charge; and clarify the conditions for obtaining artificial interruption of pregnancy in approved facilities.

Paragraph 4 of the revised legislation states that "pregnancy is artificially interrupted if the woman hands in a written application" and provided that her pregnancy does not exceed 12 weeks and there are no contradictory health indications. If the woman is under 16 years of age, the law requires the approval of her "lawful representative" or the person entrusted with her education. If the woman is between 16 and 18 years old, her "lawful representative" will be notified of the procedure by the medical facility where it was performed.

The revised legislation instructs the woman to submit her written request for pregnancy termination to a gynecologist on the staff of the health establishment to which she has been assigned according to her permanent residence, workplace, or school. The gynecologist is then obliged to inform the woman about possible effects of induced abortion on her future health, and to instruct her about efficient contraceptive practices. If the woman insists on having an abortion and the gynecologist confirms that all necessary conditions have been met, an appointment will be made to schedule the procedure. If the gynecologist believes that the necessary conditions have not been met, the woman may, within three days, file a written request for review with the district specialist in obstetrics and gynecology who is then required to consult with at least two other specialists and render a decision within two days after receipt of the appeal. If the request is approved, an appointment to schedule the procedure is made.

If the district specialist denies the woman's appeal but the woman insists on having an abortion, the district specialist must, without delay, transmit her written application to the regional specialist for re-examination. The regional specialist is obligated to consult with at least two other specialists and to render an opinion within three days of receipt of the request. If approval is granted, an appointment to schedule the procedure is made. If the request is again denied, a written statement of the reasons for the decision will be provided to the woman. There is no possibility of further appeal.

The major change in the new legislation is that the woman will be spared the potential embarrassment of appearing before an abortion commission. These have generally included as members persons unaffiliated with the health professions and charged with the responsibility of examining requests made primarily for social and economic reasons. Such an investigation often took longer, occasionally exceeding the time limit set for granting abortion on request. Henceforth, decisions must be made more quickly and are entirely in the hands of physicians. However, charges will be imposed for abortions performed for reasons other than the woman's health or defective development of the fetus.

The purpose of the new law is "to protect women's life and health and in behalf of planned and responsible parenthood," objectives shared by the Prague Cohort studies. Its effectiveness will depend, in part, on the implementation of programs designed to reduce the incidence of unwanted pregnancies.

Do the UP Children Know?

Perhaps the most frequently asked question is whether the UP children were told or eventually discovered that they were born from unwanted pregnancies. As far as the Prague Cohort study is concerned, we cannot be entirely certain. Great care was taken to preserve individual anonymity and confidentiality. The study was always described as focusing on child development. The question of abortion was raised only once — as the last item in the initial structured interview with the mothers when the children were nine years old. Responses received at that time were carefully guarded so as not to identify UP subjects to the members of the research team.

While it appears unlikely that the parents told the children about the special circumstances of their birth (38 percent of the UP women denied ever having requested abortion for this pregnancy), it could be that a few UP subjects heard about it at a time or in a context quite unrelated to the research. Only after the third follow-up was completed and the findings cited by the media in conjunction with discussions of proposals for revised abortion legislation did some of the women who had requested a procedure more than 20 years earlier recognize and recall their own experiences with the abortion commissions. How this will affect future cooperation and further follow-up only time will tell.

Comparisons with the Göteborg Cohort, 1939-42

As will be recalled from Chapter 4, the Göteborg Cohort consisted of 120 children born between 1939 and 1942 to women whose requests for abortion on psychiatric grounds had been denied by medical authorities. For each of those UP children, the very next same-sexed child born in the same hospital was selected as an AP control. No attempt was made to pair-match the children and significant differences occurred on such indicators as out-of-wedlock births, adoptions, age of mothers, number of children in the family, and socioeconomic status. Comparisons between the UP and AP group were limited to data recorded in public registers when the study participants were 20 to 21 years old. No individual interviews were conducted. Nevertheless, the findings, as shown in Table 4.2 on page 42, demonstrated that individuals born after refusal of an application for therapeutic abortion were at greater risk than the controls for adverse psychosocial problems during their developmental years. These differences tended to diminish gradually over the subsequent 15 years to age 35.

The Göteborg Cohort is comparable with the Prague Cohort only on the basis of "unwantedness" of the pregnancy. Yet, in spite of all the differences in methodology, the register findings are remarkably similar at a comparable age (about 20 years after birth). There is the same distribution and consistent drift in disfavor of the UP children. Although records of admission to psychiatric hospitals were not searched in Prague, the study participants' assessment of their own mental health in the structured interviews is also consistent with the Göteborg findings. Whether or not the differences between the UP subjects and AP controls will diminish in Prague by age 35, as they did in Göteborg, remains to be seen.

Comparisons with the 1948 Stockholm Cohort

As described in Chapter 5, *Höök* (1963) focused her work on 249 women whose applications for abortion had been refused by the Swedish National Board of Health in 1948. She searched registers, conducted free-form follow-up interviews with the women some years later, and eventually followed to age 23 the 88 UP children then residing in the Stockholm area. Taking as a paired control the same-sexed classmate with the nearest birthday, she found a preponderance of behavioral and conduct disorders in the UP boys, many of whom came from unstable homes and had never known their natural fathers. UP subjects had a higher incidence of sick leave than AP controls, appeared more often in the delinquency register, and were rated as lower in emotional maturity than would have been expected on the basis of age. However, there was no statistically significant difference in school performance as measured by post-junior high school studies.

As in the case of the Göteborg Cohort, there are important methodological differences between the studies of the 1948 Stockholm and the Prague Cohorts. Nevertheless, the delinquency register findings are in the same direction as the observations on the emotional development of the UP children when compared to the AP controls. While there were no differences on overall school performance, there may well have been on specific subjects. Subsequent follow-up studies to age 23 are similar to those reported from Prague.

Comparison with the 1960 Swedish Cohort

As described in Chapter 5, a series of studies was conducted by *Huttin* and *Ottosson* (1971), *Arfwidsson* and *Ottosson* (1971), and by *Blomberg* (1980 a, b, and c), working with case files of children born to women whose applications for abortion had been denied by the Swedish National Board of Health in 1960. They collected an AP control series by taking the woman with the immediately following case record number in the same obstetrical unit of the same hospital who had not requested an abortion. One objective was to ascertain whether fetal development is influenced by the mother's mental status and her negative attitude toward the pregnancy. The incidence of malformations, as defined by the criteria established by the Swedish Register of Malformations, was 1.8 percent in the UP subjects and 1.1 percent in the AP controls. The number of malformations increased with mother's age when combined with lower socioeconomic status in the UP group, while no such connection was found in the AP control group. The UP children had a significantly higher incidence of cleft palate than the national norm. While the total number was only four cases, *Blomberg* regarded these findings as supporting the hypothesis that emotional stress in a pregnant woman, operationally defined by the stated unwantedness of the pregnancy, may interfere with fetal development and result in a higher incidence of malformations. However, there was a significantly lower number of stillbirths in the UP group and no differences between the UP children and the AP controls in birth weight and height, in prematurity, or in neonatal or postnatal mortality rates.

Malformation assessment criteria in the Prague Cohort study were considerably different from those established by the Swedish Register. Even slight morphological deviations were noted in Prague. They were found in 40.5 percent of the UP children and 38.2 percent of the AP controls. The difference is so minimal that interpre-

120

tation would be hazardous. Similarly, only negligible differences between the groups were found in the symptomatology of minimal brain dysfunction, visual and hearing impairments, etc.

It must be recalled that a high proportion of unwanted pregnancies in both Sweden and Prague were, in fact, never delivered. Under these circumstances it can be hypothesized that those who were born constitute a relatively positive selection of the UP population and, in consequence, would be relatively free from adverse anatomical and physiological prenatal symptomatology. Embryos and fetuses which survived the UP mothers' possible attempts to induce abortion, their perhaps improper food intake, and probably negligent health care during pregnancy may to some extent appear healthier at birth than their AP control counterparts, of whom a certain proportion may have been so-called "prayed-for children," born from artificially maintained pregnancies. The Prague findings seem to suport this presumption and concur with those of *Blomberg* (see Table 6.11, page 67).

Subsequently, *Blomberg* (1980 d) examined postnatal, somatic, and psychosocial development over 15 years in 90 pairs of same-sexed UP and AP children born in the same delivery ward whose mothers were of similar age, parity, and social class. Comparisons were made on the basis of school grades, school health cards, and social welfare registers, following the method used earlier by *Forssman* and *Thuwe* (1966) and described in Chapter 4. No individual assessments or interviews of the mothers or children were conducted.

Blomberg's findings were similar to those noted by *Forssman* and *Thuwe* in Göteborg a generation earlier and, by and large, are consistent with the Prague Cohort study as well. While there were no significant differences between the UP children and the pair-matched AP controls in physical development, the UP children had significantly poorer school grades in Swedish and mathematics in their eighth year of school. They were on record as having neurotic or psychosomatic symptoms twice as often as the AP controls, were more frequently registered with the social welfare authorities, and only about half as many resided with their natural parents. Moreover, even among the 48 pairs of UP children and AP controls who lived with their natural mothers and fathers, statistically significant differences in school achievement in disfavor of the UP children persisted. Specific details are presented in Chapter 5.

Comparisons with the 1966 Northern Finland Cohort

As reported in Chapter 8, the Northern Finland study is following 12,058 children born in 1966 to women residing in the two northernmost provinces who indicated during the 24th or 28th week of gestation whether or not their pregnancies occurred at a propitious time, would have been more desirable later, or should not have occurred at all. About 96 percent of the questionnaires were completed and 12 percent of the women indicated that the pregnancy was unwanted. Most of these women did not meet the strict criteria for pregnancy termination prevailing in Finland at that time. The incidence of infant mortality, cerebral palsy, and mental retardation was significantly higher among the UP children, while family socioeconomic conditions were poorer, than for the wanted children.

Among the UP children, 300 were selected at random and pair-matched with children born from desired pregnancies. Matching criteria were based on the Prague experience. Studies were conducted when the children were eight years old and had completed the first year of compulsory education, and again at age 16, during their last compulsory year of school. Initially, there were no significant differences between the groups in overall school achievement as reflected by school grades or in relationships to teachers and peers. However, significantly more UP children required remedial teaching in reading and writing (but not in mathematics). Verbal performance, as assessed by the teachers, was significantly poorer than for the children from wanted pregnancies.

At the age of 16, a series of 88 children were pair-matched. In contrast to the Prague Cohort study, no significant differences were found among either boys or girls in their perception of their mothers. However, the UP girls perceived their fathers as more hostile, had lower school grades, and were rated less favorably by their teachers than AP controls. While the UP girls were more often reluctant to go to school and wanted to leave at the earliest possible age, perceiving their parents to be dissatisfied with them, no such differences were observed between UP boys and their controls. An explanation for these findings was sought in traditional attitudes toward boys and girls in Northern Finland.

As the Finnish study is still continuing, further results are expected. While the matching criteria are similar to those of Prague, the operational definition of "unwantedness" is somewhat different, depending on the woman's own assessment of her attitude towards the pregnancy late in gestation as compared to a twice refused application for abortion in Prague. That the findings to date are convergent suggests that "unwantedness" plays a major role in the home atmosphere, the environment in which the child lives, grows, and develops.

Concluding Observations

The Prague research as well as the diverse Scandinavian studies all tend to support the hypothesis that, in the aggregate, children born from unwanted pregnancies are at increased risk even as late as young adulthood. Most likely, this risk also involves an aggregate of factors. Presumably, there is no direct link or clear-cut connection between unwanted pregnancies and the deviations found in subsequent psychosocial development. Quite probably, these deviations result from the combined action of a whole range of adverse circumstances, beginning with the unwanted pregnancy and the denial of abortion. Perhaps only in a few cases has the unwanted pregnancy alone played the decisive part. Notwithstanding the scrupulous

122

observation of the matching criteria, the UP mothers as a group appeared socially less competent at the very beginning of the Prague study. Some applied for abortion too late. Others had had abortions before the birth of the UP child, even if not subsequently. They were more often unable to find a reliable partner for marriage, and divorced and remarried more frequently so that more of the UP than AP children had stepfathers. Under these circumstances it is very difficult to identify exactly what is the consequence of which specific factor. For purposes of practical public health policy, we suggest viewing unwantedness in early pregnancy in a global sense, that is, as reflecting and very likely foreshadowing a family atmosphere which in many instances is not conducive to healthy childrearing and likely to impact negatively on the child's subsequent psychosocial development.

One other finding deserves reiteration. While the Maladaptation Score calculated at age nine, as well as the Psychosocial Instability Score calculated at age 21-23, show highly significant differences in disfavor of the UP subjects, there is still a large proportion who are as well adapted as the great majority of AP controls. A few even scored at the extreme of positivity. What is the differentiating factor? What is it that in the fate of one child operates adversely but benignly in that of another? Are there certain coping mechanisms that transform or at least neutralize the effects of unwantedness?

Most likely, many different factors interact. In our view, the essence lies in the psychosocial significance of "unwantedness" as perceived and experienced by the mother and the marital couple. We can hypothesize that when a woman twice requested abortion for more or less "external" reasons (e.g., difficult social or emotional circumstances, poor housing, or a bad economic situation), the chances of accepting the child after birth are much greater. If her applications for abortion were motivated by deeper considerations (e.g., negative attitude toward the father, rejection of children per se, disturbance of female and maternal identity, etc.), then it is quite probable that her rejection of the pregnancy will continue in some form after she has given birth involuntarily. This hypothesis is supported by the highly significant differences noted between the UP and the AP only children. However, the ground rules of the Prague study for preserving anonymity and confidentiality limited inquiry into the reasons for requesting abortion to the material available in the files of the district and regional abortion commissions. Only a single question was asked about possible requests to interrupt this pregnancy, and just once as the final item on the initial structured interview with the mothers when their children were about nine years old. Those women who acknowledged having made such a request were then asked their present opinion of the commission's decision (and, as noted, they were not seen by the interviewer again and their anonymity was carefully preserved).

The findings accumulated from the UP subjects, born from manifestly unwanted pregnancies, operationally defined by having twice requested abortion for the same pregnancy, reflect quite clearly, in our view, a drift in a socially problematic direction that has become increasingly apparent over time in comparison with pair-matched controls. Emerging from subdeprivation, the relationships of the young UP adults with their families of origin, friends, coworkers, supervisors, and especially with their sexual or marital partners are dogged by serious difficulties. Particularly impressive is the common feature noted at age nine, at ages 14-16, and again at age 21-23: the UP subjects are not so much overrepresented on the extremely negative indicators at they are underrepresented on the positive ones. They are rarely observed on any indicator of excellence. Generally speaking, in comparison to AP controls, the UP subjects appear handicapped by a relatively slight social deviation, which may, however, have some far-reaching consequences.

The tendency of the UP subjects to develop in a socially less desirable and less accepted direction can hardly be denied. To be specific, the population of UP subjects apparently, and not accidentally, includes a larger than usual number of persons less capable of forming healthy, satisfactory, and creative emotional relations with other people in their immediate social environment. They represent a numerically strong subdeprivational potential that can lead, under certain circumstances, to serious social failures, as evidenced, for example, in alcoholism and criminal behavior. And, as suggested from the beginning of the Prague study, the family is the major area where UP subjects encounter an increased risk of failure in comparison to AP controls who do not suffer from the handicap of subdeprivation.

In conclusion, the findings of the Prague study — and also of the Scandinavian research — lend reasonable support to the hypothesis that insufficient gratification of basic social and emotional needs (which accompanies many UP children from early childhood) tends to create an unfavorable social environment with negative effects in personality development, social relations, and self-realization. Whether or not this tendency will affect the next generation only time will tell.

Abortion Policy Suggestions

As noted in the Overview (Chapter 1, page 10), the worldwide legal status of abortion ranges from complete prohibition (which may or may not be enforced) to elective procedures as the request of the pregnant woman. We are particularly concerned about those countries where abortion may be legally available but not readily accessible to women in need, and that part of the world where abortion is either still illegal for any reason, or permitted only on narrowly defined grounds to protect the woman's life or health. Our concern arises from the observation that in countries with rather strict limits on the technical availability and practical accessibility of legal abortion, there is usually very little consideration of the psychological condition of the pregnant woman, that is, her readiness to accept a maternal role.

The ambivalence about their pregnancy reported by a large proportion of the UP women has already been noted. These women can be further divided into essentially three groups, reflecting different initial perceptions and subsequent behavior. The first group includes those who requested abortion for primarily temporary so-

124

cioeconomic reasons, mostly housing and financial conditions which were not deemed conducive to ensuring a good family life at that time. After overcoming their social problems, these women generally accepted their pregnancies and adapted to their maternity within a reasonably short time. Subsequently, few differences were noted between this group of UP women and the AP controls who had accepted their pregnancies from the beginning.

A second group consists of those UP women who were unmarried, had a transient love affair, or lived in a situation of major marital conflict. Acceptance of pregnancy and adaptation to maternity was much more difficult for them and often nearly impossible. In these cases, difficult interpersonal relations may lead to emotional and existential uncertainty and, as one result, the negative attitudes toward the natural father or marital partner are reflected in attitudes toward the child. This group may also include a further subgroup of very young, emotionally immature women who decided to marry during the pregnancy but divorced soon after delivery and subsequently changed marital status several times.

The third group includes women incapable of accepting a maternal role because of deep-seated intrapersonal problems. They can be quite good lovers and wives, but not mothers. When compelled by circumstances to give birth involuntarily, such a woman may appear to others as expressing positive views which, in actuality, are rather superficial and mask a basically negative attitude to motherhood. She does not want a child because she does not perceive any maternal feelings within herself, but is reluctant to admit the lack of such emotions.

Abortion commissions or individuals in a position to approve or deny a request for termination of an unwanted pregnancy are seldom aware of, sensitive to, or even interested in the psychological rationale which is often the basis of the woman's decision. Moreover, adequate resources may not be available for making a determination of the woman's actual and perceived life situation within a fairly short period of time. Psychological counseling can seldom be provided and referral to other community facilities may conflict with the time pressure for a decision.

In sum, the Prague experience suggests that the final decision about abortion should be the right of the woman alone, assuming that there are no contraindicating health reasons. If our study demonstrates, as we believe, that unwantedness constitutes a certain risk for the subsequent social development of children and young adults, then everything possible should be done to reduce the incidence of not only unwanted pregnancies but also of children born involuntarily.

Suggestions for Future Research and Education

Just as the Prague studies have considered unwanted pregnancies from different perspectives, so our suggestions will also be addressed to different facets, ranging from future research directions to public health policy and education for responsible parenthood.

We are most hopeful that the Prague Study will be continued. If given the opportunity, we wish to explore what kind of parents the original UP children have become, which sort of influences their partners have had, and whether or not the longer term effects of unwantedness cast a shadow on the next generation. The findings collected thus far form the very small pilot sample of married UP men and women and AP controls, reported on page 100, encourage continued research. And, of course, we would wish to learn whether the significant differences between the UP subjects and AP controls noted through ages 21-23 will diminish by age 35, as reported from Sweden (*Forssman* and *Thuwe* in Chapter 4).

Also urgently needed are studies of the development of parent-child relationships. We have repeatedly called attention to the importance of compensating mechanisms which seem to be conducive to transforming an originally negative attitude to pregnancy into a positive attitude to the child born involuntarily. Very little is known about how these mechanisms work. We specifically suggest implementation of prospective studies beginning with early pregnancy and continuing through the first two or three years of life. The current methodology of assessing the family, parents, and the child should be supplemented by indicators of family interaction and by more extensive study of the father. Much can be learned by consulting with colleagues in other countries who have been involved in related research.

From a social and public health perspective, major emphasis should be on the prevention of unwanted pregnancies. To be successful, this objective should be shared and implemented by society as a whole, involving multiple available resources both governmental and nongovernmental. The basic approach will perhaps focus on purposive goal-directed education, beginning well before puberty and encouraging acceptance of the concept of responsible parenthood and the obligations it implies. This means going beyond traditional sexuality education and all the cautions imposed by the threat of AIDS to a greater appreciation of the meaning of parenthood and the satisfactions of emotional needs that wanted children can provide. Ideally, incorporating such an approach to sexual life will result in establishing more mature partner relationships, creating an emotional atmosphere conducive to healthy child development, and having a positive impact upon society as a whole.

The Prague studies suggest that several specific components be included in the integrated educational endeavor. The UP children, their mothers, and probably their fathers as well, showed considerable deficiency in their social interactions with others. Preventive efforts, aimed at making children more aware of their social interactions, should be initiated at a preschool age. Children should be taught to cooperate and draw satisfaction from cooperation, assert their initiative while respecting the needs of others, and understand conflict and positive conflict resolution.

Similarly, education for responsible parenthood must go beyond establishing healthy feminine and masculine identities to fostering joint responsibilities and the ability to experience life with a partner as a creative process. The Prague studies indicate that knowledge about and mastery of birth control techniques do not assure prevention of unwanted pregnancies unless reproductive behavior is based on the joint decision that one partner will actively assume responsibility. Such an approach will enhance the positive aspects of a planned and well-timed pregnancy likely to bring maximal satisfaction to the marital partners, contribute to their personality growth, and encourage a family environment conducive to healthy child development.

The findings reported from Prague are consistent with numerous studies of psychological deprivation and substitutional child care. Children appear to develop better in an atmosphere in which the parents derive personal satisfaction from their parental roles. Joyful childhood and joyful parenthood reinforce each other. Involuntary parenthood rarely provides the best social environment for the child, nor the most stimulating educational setting. This message should become ingrained in educational programs and directed toward the public through more skillful use of the mass media, especially television. Parents who are emotionally mature and responsible, psychosexually well attuned to each other, and also happy in their family life are the best guarantee of fostering similar attitudes in their children, thus hopefully reducing the incidence of future unwanted pregnancies and resort to abortion.

Chapter 10

Sources of Data and Research Methods Used in the Prague Study

---

STAGE ONE

Children

1. *Delivery Records*
Contain basic information on the history of the pregnancy and the delivery and the condition of the baby at birth, including weight and length.

2. *The Records of the Pediatric Outpatient Clinic and the School Health Service*
Contain assessments of the physical development of the child during the first six years of life, including all illnesses, accidents, defects, etc., which required a physician's visit or other medical attention.

3. *The Case History*
Developed by an experienced social worker from a direct interview with the mother.

4. *Physical Examination of Child*
Detailed physical examination of the child conducted by an experienced pediatrician from the Child Psychiatric Service. It determined the current state of the child's health, physical maturity, motor capabilities, laterality, and functioning of the sensory organs and the nervous system. Special attention was paid to symptoms of minimal brain dysfunction.

5. *Psychological Examination of Child*
The psychological examination of the child included six separate testing methods:
a) *Wechsler Intelligence Scale for Children* (1955).
b) *Bene-Anthony Test of Family Relations* (1957).
c) *Aspiration-Frustration Test.* Adapted from a method used in clinical practice. It consists of a board with holes into which the child places his "mushrooms." Nine experiments are conducted. Before each of them, the child is asked to estimate

128

how many mushrooms can be put into place in 30 seconds, which is the time limit of the first four experiments. In the fifth through eigh experiments, however, the child is allowed to place only half the number of mushrooms he has to work with and is told that his time is up. The ninth experiment again has a time limit of 30 seconds. A number of indicators are assessed, especially the child's reaction to frustration in the second part of the test.

d) *Drawing of the Family.* A projective technique used in clinical practice. Instructions: "Draw a picture which expresses the life of your whole family." The assessment scale was specially adapted for the purpose of this study.

e) *Story Completion Test.* Two stories from a set developed by *Geisler* (1956) and three new stories adapted for the study.

f) *Structured Interview with the Child.* Contains five questions aimed at eliciting information on the relationship between the child and the family and the child's desires and fears.

g) *Sociometric Examination.* Conducted with all children in the class which the UP or AP child attends. The children are given a list of nine traits and asked to fill in names of their classmates whom they consider to be most typical of them.

h) *Rating Scale of the Personal Traits of the Child.* An assessment scale containing 12 traits. The extent to which the child has a specific trait is expressed by a five-point scale. Each child is assessed independently by the mother, her husband, and the teacher. The teacher is also given a 15-item assessment scale, on which the UP child is directly compared with the AP control child.

i) *Child's Behavior During Psychological Testing.* A four-point rating scale assessing the degree of communication between the child and the examiner, ability to cooperate, make a concentrated effort, etc.

Mothers

1. The original request of the mother for an induced abortion and the case record of the district and appellate commissions which rejected her request.

2. *Delivery Records*

3. *Case History Interview with Mother*

Completed by an experienced social worker, the form contains 56 items. Mothers' statements are classified according to qualitative or quantitative criteria.

4. *Structured Interview with Mother*

The model for the interview was developed especially for this study. A questionnaire with scaled questions is submitted to the mother individually. It assesses her opinions of and conscious attitudes toward her child, herself, her spouse, and her family life. The number of questions and their sequence are standard.

5. *"Aims in Life" Questionnaire*

Part of the BOD questionnaire by *Kratochvíl* (1973), it contains 15 "aims in life which people try to achieve." The person examined is asked to choose five aims that he or she considers most important. The degree of importance is indicated by attaching the numbers one to five to the aims selected by each respondent.

6. *"H2" Questionnaire*

Two sets of questions are used to evaluate the respondent's optimism about his/her life and trust in his/her social environment.

7. *Eysenck's EPI Questionnaire* (1964) (Czech adaptation EOD, 1968).

8. *Bene-Anthony Test of Family Relations Modified for Parents*

From the same test given to children, 15 items were selected of which five indicate positive relations between mother and child, five indicate negative relations, and five indicate a mother's overprotectiveness of the child. This list was submitted to the mother, who was asked to respond to each item the way she thought her child would.

9. *"MŽ" Questionnaire* (femine and masculine identity)

A questionnaire constructed for the purposes of this study, it was used only with a subgroup of the mothers and processed separately.

10. *PARI Questionnaire* by *Schaefer* and *Bell* (1958)

Used only with a subgroup of the mothers and processed separately.

11. *Impression of Interview with Mother*

A rating scale devised for this study, it assesses the mother's view of herself, her child, and her spouse, how truthful her answers were, and the degree of knowledge about her child. Assessment is made independently by a social worker and a psychiatrist.

STAGE TWO

1. *Questionnaire I*

Sent out to the parents of the UP and AP children, its six items provide basic information about the child's school career, occupation, and the parents' social status.

2. *School Questionnaire*

Used in the first stage of the research, it was completed by teachers and provides data on the child's school achievement, personal qualities, the teacher's view of the child's family, etc.

3. *Rating Scale of Child's Personal Traits*

Twelve qualities on a five-point scale are rated by each child's mother and class teacher. (Identical with that used in the first stage of the research).

4. Questionnaire for Youth: Childhood-Marriage-Family

Developed for this stage of the research, it was completed by each child individually. Its 35 items deal with the child's childhood memories, views of love, sexual, and partner relations, and family life, including aboriton, divorce, etc.

5. Schludermanns' CRPBI Questionnaire (1970) (Czech version ADOR, 1983)

The Czech version of CRPBI has five subscales: mother's and father's positive interest in the child, authoritarian attitude, hostility toward the child, autonomy granted the child, and parental inconsistency. Two additional scores are calculated: score of positivity (parental positivity minus hostility) and score of authoritarianism (authoritarianism minus autonomy). Each child completed the questionnaire individually.

6. PAQ

This questionnaire designed by *Rohner* (1980) assesses subjects' character traits on seven scales (aggressiveness, dependency, feelings of inferiority concerning their own character and abilities, emotional stability, ability to respond emotionally, and optimistic or pessimistic outlook on life).

STAGE THREE

1. Questionnaire I

Enclosed with the first letter sent to renew contact, it sought to obtain basic information about current occupation, marital status, educational status, number of children (if any), military service (for men), and housing.

2. Questionnaire DM

Sent out to mothers of the subjects together with an explanatory letter, the questions inquired about the mother's current family situation, her relationship with the child studied, and satisfaction with the child's job, education, emotional relationships, social position, etc.

3. Questionnaire for Youth: Childhood-Marriage-Family

Mailed to the subjects, it had been designed for this study and first used in Stage Two. The subject assesses his or her childhood and education, including views of sexual and partner relationships, family life, education, divorces, induced abortions, etc.

4. Schludermanns' CRPBI Questionnaire (Czech version ADOR)

Also sent to the subjects by mail, the Czech version (*Matějček* and *Říčan*, 1983) asks each subject to assess the educational patterns of his or her father and mother at the time when the child was about 12 to 13 years of age.

A third letter informed the subjects about the further program of the study and reminded them that they would be invited for an individual interview.

The following methods were employed during the individual meetings or during visits by project researchers to the families of the subjects.

5. *Interview with Each Young Adult*

Originally devised for this stage of the study, the interview includes 60 questions with scaled answers concerning each subject's relationships with the family of origin, job, superiors and co-workers, relationships with friends and peers, etc. The largest part is devoted to emotional and sexual relations, perceptions of marriage, knowledge of his/her development etc. The list was extended by several questions about life style, concluding with the request to assess the degree of life satisfaction up to this point in time. The structured interview is the main source of information at this stage of the study.

Additional questionnaires were completed by the subjects during the individual interview and subsequently reviewed item by item with each.

6. *DZČ Questionnaire*

DZČ is a supplement to the previous interview, inquiring about subjects' leisure time, their interests, hobbies, etc.

7. *RP-PARQ*

Rohner's questionnaire (1980), based on the theory of "parental acceptance and rejection" of the child (PART), asks each subject to assess the parents' educational techniques and attitudes on four scales (emotional warmth, hostility, neglect, and rejection).

8. *DOPEN*

Eysenck's personality questionnaire EPQ (1976), adapted by *Ruisel* and *Müllner* (1982), asks each subject to rate his/her character traits on three dimensions: neuroticism, extroversion-introversion, and psychoticism.

9. *STAI*

Spielberger's questionnaire of anxiety and neurotic features (1970), adapted by *Müllner, Ruisel,* and *Farkaš* (1980).

10. *Impression from Interview*

A rating scale of 12 items, each with four points of intensity, was used by the visiting social worker to express quantitatively her impressions from contact with the subject and his or her family environment.

In addition, married UP and AP men and women were asked by the visiting social worker to complete two "values in life" questionnaires:

11. *"Aims in Life" Questionnaire*

Part of the BOD questionnaire devised by *Kratochvíl* (1973) for purposes of psychiatric diagnosis (identical with that used with mothers in Stage One of this study), it consists of 15 life aims people try to achieve. The subject is asked to choose five he or she regards as most important and to indicate the order of importance.

12. MŽ Questionnaire

Devised specifically for this study and used first with mothers in Stage One of this study, its purpose is to record male and female identity, i.e., the way women and men come to terms with their roles in life and how they assess them. The questionnaire has five sections: (1) satisfaction with female-male roles, (2) disadvantages of the female role, (3) factors causing mutual attraction of sexes, (4) order of importance within individual components of the male and the female role, and (5) whether the subject would again choose his or her sex if a choice could be made.

Married subjects with children were further investigated by the visiting social worker with the help of these methods:

13. RM/RO II

The plan of the interview with the mother and father of the child, devised for the purposes of this study, included 17 items with scaled responses. The interview focused on the parents' readiness for the child's birth, their attitudes toward the child, outlook for the future, etc.

14. Case History of the Child

The case history interview with the mother (who may be a UP or AP child) contains 123 items, noting the family-tree and developmental, educational, familial and social history, including the economic and housing situation of the family.

15. RM/RO I

The plan of the interview was adapted for this stage of the study from previously used questionnaires. It includes 22 items with scaled answers, investigating the parents' mutual relations, their educational methods and views, and knowledge of the child's development. The last item is "attitude toward pregnancy." It is presented to these young wives and husbands with the same wording used with their parents 11 or 12 years earlier. Among other things, the interview allows computing an agreement score between the answers given by the father and mother.

16. Attitude Toward the Child

A rating scale of seven items with five points, constructed for the purposes of this stage of the study, asks each researcher to quantitatively express an impression of the mother's and father's attitudes toward the child as gained during the interview with each.

Chapter 11

References and Related Readings

Anthony, E. J., Benedek, T. (1970). *Parenthood: Its psychology and psychopathology*. London, Little Brown.

Aren, P., Amark, C. (1961). The prognosis in cases in which legal abortion has been granted but not carried out. *Acta Psychiatrica Scandinavica*, 36, 203-278.

Arfwidsson, L., Ottosson, J. O. (1971). Pregnancy and delivery of unwanted children. *Acta Psychiatrica Scandinavica*, Supplement 221, 77-83.

Ariès, P. (1960). *L'enfant et la vie familiale sous l'ancient régime*. Paris, Librairie Plon.

Ariès, P. (1969). Le rôle nouveau de la mére et de l'enfat dans la famille moderne. *UNICEF, Les Carnets de l'Enfance*, 10.

Beck, M. B. (1959). The destiny of the unwanted child: The issue of compulsory pregnancy. In C. Reiterman (Ed.), *Abortion and the unwanted child*. The California Committee on Therapeutic Abortion. New York, International Universities Press, 14.

Beck, M. B. (1970). Abortion: The mental health consequences of unwantedness. *Seminars of Psychiatry*, 2, 263-274.

Bene, E., Anthony, J. (1957). *Manual for Family Relation Test*. London, National Foundation for Educational Research in England and Wales.

Blomberg, S. (1980a). Influence of maternal distress during pregnancy on fetal development and mortality. *Acty Psychiatrica Scandinavica*, 62, 298-314.

Blomberg, S. (1980b). Influence of maternal distress during pregnancy on fetal malformations. *Acta Psychiatrica Scandinavica*, 62, 315-330.

Blomberg, S. (1980c). Influence of maternal distress during pregnancy on complications in pregnancy and delivery. *Acta Psychiatrica Scandinavica*, 62, 399-404.

Blomberg, S. (1980d). Influence of maternal distress during pregnancy on postnatal development. *Acta Psychiatrica Scandinavica*, 62, 405-417.

Bohman, S. (1970). *Adopted children and their families*. Stockholm, Proprius.

Bohman, S. (1971). A comparative study of adopted children and children in their biological environment born after undesired pregnancies. *Acta Paediatrica Scandinavica*, Supplement 221.

Bowlby, J. (1969). *Attachment and loss*. London, Hogarth Press.

Brody, S. (1956). *Patterns of mothering*. New York, International Universities Press.

Bumpass, L. L., Westoff, C. F. (1970). The "perfect contraceptive" population. *Science*, 169, 1177-1182.

Burch, T. K. (1980). Decision-making theories in demography: an introduction. In T. K. Burch (Ed.), *Interdisciplinary perspective on decision-making*. Boulder, Westview Press.

Callahan, D. (1970). *Abortion: Law, choice, and morality*. New York, MacMillan.

Campbell, A. A. (1969). Family planning and the five million. *Family Planning Perspectives*, 1, 33-36.

Caplan, B. (1954). The disturbance of mother-child relationship by unsuccessful attempts at abortion. *Mental Hygiene*, 38, 67-80.

Chen, P. C. (1970). China's birth control action programme 1956-1964. *Population Studies*, 24, 141-158.

Connecticut. (1821). *The public statute laws of the state of Connecticut*, 1921, 151-153. Hartford.

Couzinet, B., Lestrat, N., Ulmann, A., Baulieu, E. E., Schaison, G. (1986). Termination of early pregnancy by the progesterone antagonist RU 486 (mifepristone). *The New England Journal of Medicine*, 315, 1566-1570.

134

David, H. P. (1970). *Family planning and abortion in the socialist countries of Central and Eastern Europe.* New York, The Population Council, 161-196.

David, H. P. (1971). Mental health and family planning. *Family Planning Perspectives,* 3, 20-23.

David, H. P. (1972). Unwanted pregnancies: Costs and alternatives. In C. F. Westoff, R. Parke, Jr. (Eds.), *Demographic and social aspects of population growth.* Vol. 1 of the Commission on Population Growth and the American Future Research reports. Washington, DC, US Government Printing Office, 439-466.

David, H. P. (1973a). Abortion seeking behavior in Eastern Europe. *American Journal of Orthopsychiatry,* 42, 284.

David, H. P. (1973b). Abortion trands in European socialist countries and in the U.S.A. *American Journal of Orthopsychiatry,* 43, 376.

David, H. P. (1973c). Psychological studies in abortion. In J. T. Fawcett (Ed.), *Psychological perspectives on population.* New York, Basic Books, 241-273.

David, H. P. (Ed.) (1974a). *Abortion research: International experience.* Lexington, Mass. Health.

David, H. P. (1974b). Abortion and family planning in the Soviet Union: Public and private behaviour. *Journal of Biosocial Science,* 6, 417-426.

David, H. P. (1978). Psychosocial studies of abortion in the United States. In H. P. David, H. L. Friedman, J. van der Tak, and M. Sevilla (Eds.). *Abortion in psychosocial perspective: Trends in transnational research.* New York, Springer, 77-115.

David, H. P. (1980). The abortion decision: National and international perspectives. In J. T. Burtcheall (Ed.). *Abortion parley.* Kansas City, Andrews and McMeel.

David, H. P. (1981a). Abortion policies. In J. E. Hodgson (Ed.), *Abortion and sterilization: Medical and social aspects.* London, Academic Press, 1-40.

David, H. P. (1981b). Unwantedness: Longitudinal studies of Prague children born to women twice denied abortion for the same pregnancy and matched controls. In P. Ahmed (Ed.), *Coping with medical issues: Pregnancy, childbirth, and parenthood.* New York, Elsevier, 81-102.

David, H. P. (1982a). Induced abortion: Psychosocial perspectives. In J. W. Sciara (Ed.), *Gynaecology and obstetrics.* Philadelphia, Harper and Row.

David, H. P. (1982b). Eastern Europe: Pronatalist policies and private behavior. *Population Bulletin,* 36, No. 6.

David, H. P. (1983). Cuba: Low fertility high abortion. *Intercom,* 11 (7/8), 5-6.

David, H. P. (1986a). Unwanted children: A follow-up from Prague. *Family Planning Perspectives,* 18, 143-144.

David, H. P. (1986b). Population development and reproductive behavior. *American Psychologist,* 41, 309-312.

David, H. P. (1987). *Family planning for the mentally ill und handicapped.* Bethesda: Transnational Family Research Institute, 1987.

David, H. P. (1987). Family planning for the mentally ill and handicapped. In M. Osler and H. P. David (Eds.), *Sexuality, family planning and people with mental illness and handicaps.* Copenhagen, Danish Family Planning Association.

David, H. P., Baldwin, W. H. (1979). Childbearing and child development: Demographic and psychosocial trends. *American psychologist,* 34, 866-871.

David, H. P., Friedman, H. L. (1973). Psychosocial research in abortion: A transnational perspective. In H. J. Osofsky, J. D. Osofsky (Eds.), *The abortion experience: Psychological and medical impact.* Hagerstown, Harper and Row, 310-337.

David, H. P., Lindner, M. A. (1975). Family planning for the mentally handicapped. *Bulletin of the World Health Organization,* 52, 155-161.

David, H. P., Matějček, Z. (1981). Children born to women denied abortion: An update. *Family Planning Perspectives,* 13, 32-34.

David, H. P., Matějček, Z., Dytrych, Z., Schüller, V., Friedman, H. L. (1977). Developmental consequences of unwanted pregnancies: Studies from Sweden and Czechoslovakia. In Y. H. Poortinga (Ed.), *Basic problems in cross-cultural psychology.* Amsterdam, Swets and Zeitlinger, 184-189.

David, H. P., McIntyre, R. J. (1981). *Reproductive behavior: Central and Eastern European experiences.* New York, Springer.

David, H. P., Rasmussen, N. Kr. (1980). *Danish experience with effects of liberalized abortion.* Final report to CPR/NICHD (HD-09739). Bethesda and Copenhagen, Transnational Family Research Institute and Institute of Social Medicine.

David, H. P., Wright, N. H. (1971). Abortion legislation: The Romanian experience. *Studies in Family Planning,* 2, 205-210.

Davis, G. (1974). *Interception of pregnancy.* London, Angus and Robertson.

Dellapenna, J. W. (1979). The history of abortion: Technology, morality, and the law. *University of Pittsburgh Law Review,* 40, 359-428.

Dickens, B. M. (1966). *Abortion and the law.* Bristol, MacGibbon and Kee.
Dickinson, R. L., Bryant, L. F. S. (1938). *Control of conception: A clinical medical manual.* Baltimore, Williams and Wilkins.
Diggory, F. (1971): The unwanted pregnancy. *Journal of Biosocial Science,* Supplement 3, 127-132.
Dunovský, J. (1966). Statistic data in adoption in ČSSR in 1975-1964. (In Czech.) *Československá pediatrie,* 21, 170-178.
Dytrych, Z. (1970). Psychological aspects of abortion in Czechoslovakia. *Journal of Psychiatric Nursing,* 8, 4.
Dytrych, Z., Matějček, Z., Schüller, V. (1975). *Unwanted children.* (In Czech.) Zprávy VÚPs, Praha, VÚPs.
Dytrych, Z., Matějček, Z., Schüller, V., David, H. P., Friedman, H. L. (1975). Children born to women denied abortion. *Family Planning Perspectives,* 7, 165-171.
Dytrych, Z., Matějček, Z., Schüller, V. (1976). Unwanted pregnancies: Effects on mothers and children. *PHP Magazine,* Tokyo, 7, 2-12.
Dytrych, Z. Matějček, Z., Schüller, V. (1986). Psychosocial development of children born from unwanted pregnancies. Workshop: *Life styles, contraception, and parenthood.* Amsterdam, 25-27, Sept. 1986.
Eckard, E. (1980). Wanted and unwanted births reported by mothers 15-44 years of age: United States, 1976. *Advance data from vital and health statistics of the National Center for Health Statistics,* No. 56.
Eysenck, H. J., Eysenck, S. B. G. (1968). *Personality questionnaire EOD.* (In Czech.) Bratislava, Psychodiagnostika.
Eysenck, H. J., Eysenck, S. B. G. (1964). *Manual of the Eysenck Personality Inventory.* San Diego, University of London Press.
Eysenck, H. J., Eysenck, S. B. G. (1976). *Manual of the EPQ.* London, Hodder and Staughton.
Fawcett, J. T. (1970). *Psychology and population.* New York, The Population Council.
Fawcett, J. T. (1983). Perception of the value of children: Satisfactions and costs. In R. A. Bulatao, R. D. Lee (Eds.), *Determinants of fertility in developing countries.* New York, Academic Press, 429-457.
Festinger, L. (1957). *A theory of cognitive dissonance.* Stanford, Stanford University Press.
Field, M. G. (1956). The re-legalization of abortion in Soviet Russia. *New England Journal of Medicine.* 255, 421-427.
Fleck, S. (1964). Family welfare, mental health, and birth control. *Journal of Family Law,* 3, 241-247.
Ford, C. V., Castelnuovo-Tadesco, P., Long, K. D. (1972). Women who seek therapeutic abortion: A comparison with women who complete their pregnancies. *American Journal of Psychiatry,* 129, 58-64.
Forssman, H., Thuwe, I. (1966). One hundred and twenty children born after application for therapeutic abortion refused. *Acta Psychiatrica Scandinavica,* 42, 71—88.
Forssman, H., Thuwe, I. (1981). Continued follow-up study of 120 persons born after refusal of application for therapeutic abortion. *Acta Psychiatrica Scandinavica,* 64, 142-146.
Freedman, R., Whelpton, P. K., and Campbell, A. A. (1959). *Family planning, sterility, and population growth.* New York, McGraw-Hill.
Freud, S. (1898). Sexuality in the etiology of the neuroses. (In German.) *Wiener klinische Rundschau,* No. 2, 4, 5, and 7. Also in collected papers, New York, Basic Books, 1959, Vol. 1, 238.
Friedman, H. L., Edstrom, K. G. (1983). *Adolescent reproductive health: An approach to planning health service research.* Geneva, WHO (WHO offset publication No. 77).
Geisler, E. (1956). Projektive Testmethoden als Hilfsmittel bei der psychiatrichen Exploration von Kindern in Psychiatrie. *Neurologie und Medizinische Psychologie,* 8/7.
Gordon, L. (1976). *Woman's body, woman's right.* New York, Grossman/Viking.
Guttmacher, A. F. (1967). Unwanted pregnancy: A challenge to mental health. *Mental Hygiene,* 51, 512-516.
Harmsen, H. (1950). Notes on abortion and birth control in Germany. *Population Studies,* 3, 402-405.
Himes, N. E. (1936). *Medical history of contraception.* Baltimore, Williams and Wilkins.
Hodge, H. L. (1869). *Foeticide or criminal abortion.* Philadelphia, Lindsay and Blakiston.
Höök, K. (1963). Refused abortion: A follow-up study of 249 women whose applications were refused by the National Board of Health in Sweden. *Acta Psychiatrica Scandinavica,* Supplementum 168, Vol. 39.
Höök, K. (1971a). Depression in unwanted children. *Proceedings of the 4th U.E.P. Congress,* Stockholm, 116-125.
Höök, K. (1971b). The right of abortion. (In Swedish.) *Statens offentliga utredningar.* 1971, no. 58, 54-56,

Höök, K. (1972). The question of abortion. (In Swedish.) *Statens offentliga utredningar,* 1972, no. 39.
Höök, K. (1975). The unwanted child: Effects on mothers and children of refused applications for abortion. In: *Society, Stress, and Disease.* Oxford Medical Publications, Vol. 2, 187-192.
Höök, K. (1987). The unwanted child. A follow-up study. *Paper in preparation for Acta Psychiatrica Scandinavica.* Personal communication.
Hultin, M., Ottosson, J. O. (1971). Pregnancy and perinatal conditions of unwanted children. *Acta Psychiatrica Scandinavica,* Supplementum 221, 59-76.
Hurni, M. (1981). *Interruption de la grossesse: grossesse-non-désirée: 15 ans après.* These. Faculté de Médecine, Université de Lausanne, Lausanne.
International Planned Parenthood Federation. (1986). *Annual Report,* 1985, London, I-P-P-F.
Janis, I. C., Mann, L. (1977). *Decision making: A psychological analysis of conflict, choice, and commitment.* New York: Free Press.
Järvinen, P. A. (1971). Legal abortions in Finland. *Annales Chirurgiae et Gynaecologiae Fenniae,* 60, 65-66.
Jonsson, L. (1976). Law and fertility in Sweden. In M. Kirk, M. Livi Bacci, and E. Szabady, *Law and fertility in Europe.* Dolhain, Ordina, Vol. 2, 544-565.
Kapor-Stanulovic, N., Friedman, H. L. (1978). Studies in choice behavior in Yugoslavia. In H. P. David, H. L. Friedman, J. van der Tak, M. J. Sevilla (Eds.), *Abortion in psychosocial perspective: Trends in transnational research.* New York, Springer, 119-144.
Kellerhals, J., Wirth, G. (1972). Social dynamics of abortion request. Some considerations and preliminary results. *International Mental Health Research Newsletter,* 14, 1, 3-5.
Klackenberg, G. (1971). A prospective longitudinal study of children. *Acta Psychiatrica Scandinavica,* Supplementum 224.
Kohoutek, F., Kohoutek, M. (1974). Psychosexual problems in relation to artificial interruption of pregnancy. (In Czech.) *Československá gynekologie,* 39, 206-207.
Kohoutek, M., Křivánková, M. (1970). Destiny of women whose application for artificial interruption of pregnancy was denied. (In Czech.) *Československá gynekologie,* 35, 340.
Kratochvíl, S. (1973). *BOD.* (In Czech.) Bratislava, Psychodiagnostika.
Krchová, M. (1971). Pregnancy interruption law and its impact on population development. (In Czech.) *Zprávy populační komise,* 2-3, 52-54.
Langmeier, J., Matějček, Z. (1975). *Psychological deprivation in childhood.* New York, Wiley, Halsted Press.
Lee, L. T. (1973). International status of abortion legislation. In H. J. Osofsky and J. D. Osofsky (Eds.), *The abortion experience: Psychological and medical impact.* Hagerstown, Harper and Row Medical Department, 338-364.
Lieberman, E. J. (1964). Preventive psychiatry and family planning. *Journal of Marriage and the Family,* 26, 471-477.
Lister, J. (1867). On the antiseptic principle in the practice of surgery. *Lancet,* 2, 353-356, 668-669.
Luker, K. (1975). *Taking chances: Abortion and the decision not to contracept.* Berkeley, University of California Press.
Luker, K. (1984). *Abortion and the politics of motherhood.* Berkeley, University of California Press.
Matějček, Z. (1981). Children in families of alcoholics. (In Czech.) *Psychologia a patopsychologia dieťaťa,* 16, 303-318, 530-550.
Matějček, Z., David, H. P., Stupková, E., Schüller, V., Dytrych, Z., Jelínková, V. (1972). Prague study on children born from unwanted pregnancies. In F. J. Mönks et al. (Eds.), *Determinants of Behavioral Development.* New York, Academic Press, 593-596.
Matějček, Z., Dytrych, Z., Stupková, E., Schüller, V., David, H. P. (1970). Studies on unwanted and wanted children. In H. P. David, J. Bernheim (Eds.), *Proceedings of the conference on psychosocial factors in transnational family planning research.* Geneva, April, 28-30, 1970, AIR, Washington.
Matějček, Z., Dytrych, Z., Schüller, V. (1975). Prague study of children born from unwanted pregnancies. (In Czech.) *Psychologia a patopsychologia dieťaťa,* 10, 229-246, 292-306.
Matějček, Z., Dytrych, Z., Schüller, V. (1976). Prague study of children born from unwanted pregnancies. (In Czech.) *Psychologia a patopsychologia dieťaťa,* 11, 99-112.
Matějček, Z., Dytrych, Z., Schüller, V., Fischlová, V. (1977). Unwanted gravidity and its social psychological consequences. In A. Doležal, J. Gutvirth (Eds.), *Anthropology of maternity.* Praha, Universitas Carolina Pragensis, 321-326.
Matějček, Z., Dytrych, Z., Schüller, V. (1978a). Children from unwanted pregnancies. *Acta Psychiatrica Scandinavica,* 57, 67-90.
Matějček, Z., Dytrych, Z., Schüller, V. (1978b). Children born to women denied abortion in Czechoslovakia. In H. P. David, H. L. Friedman et al. (Eds.), *Abortion in psychosocial perspective: Trends in transnational research.* New York, Springer, 201-224.
Matějček, Z., Dytrych, Z., Schüller, V. (1979a). The Prague study of children born from unwanted pragnancies. *International Journal of Mental Health,* 7, 63-77.

Matějček, Z., Dytrych, Z., Schüller, V. (1979b). Sviluppo psicologico di bambini nati da donne cui e'stato negato l'aborto. In F. Angeli (Ed.), *Aspetti biosociali dello sviluppo.* Vol. 1, Milano, 219-222.

Matějček, Z., Dytrych, Z., Schüller, V. (1980). Follow-up study of children born from unwanted pregnancies. *International Journal of Behavioural Development,* 3, 243-251.

Matějček, Z., Dytrych, Z., Schüller, V. (1985). Follow-up study of children born to women denied abortion. In R. Porter, M. O'Connor (Eds.), *Abortion: Medical progress and social implications.* (CIBA Foundation Symposium 115.) London, Pitman, 136-149.

Matějček, Z., Dytrych, Z., Schüller, V. (1986). Enfants nés d'une grossesse non désirée. Vingt ans après. *Médecine et Hygiène,* 44, 2869-2873.

Matějček, Z., Dytrych, Z., Schüller, V. (1987). Kinder aus unerwünschten Schwangerschaften. *Der Kinderartz,* 18, 336-345.

Matějček, Z., Říčan, P. (1983). *ADOR.* (In Czech.) Bratislava, Psychodiagnostika.

Matějček, Z., Topičová, K. (1976). Child in family. (In Czech.) *Psychologia a patopsychologia dieťaťa,* 11, 311-319.

Means, C. C. (1968). The law of New York concerning abortion and the status of the foetus, 1664-1968: A case of cessation of constitutionality. *New York Law Forum,* 14, 411-514.

Means, C. C. (1970). A historian's view. In R. Hall (Ed.), *Abortion in a changing world.* Vol. 1, 16-24, Vol. 2, 137-142. New York, Columbia University Press.

Means, C. C. (1971). The Phoenix of abortional freedom: Is a penumbral or ninth amendment right about to arise from the nineteenth century legislative ashes of a fourteenth century common-law liberty? *New York Law Forum,* 17, 335-410.

Mejsnarová, B. (1977). The comparison of some socio-cultural factors in the up-bringing of children born from unwanted gravidities. Analysis of anthropometric characteristics of children born from unwanted gravidities. In A. Doležal, J. Gutvirth (Eds.), *Anthropology of maternity.* Praha, Universitas Carolina Pragensis, 327-334.

Menninger, K. (1943). Psychiatric aspects of contraception. *Bulletin of the Menninger Clinic,* 7, 36-40.

Millar, W. M. (1934). Human abortion. *Human Biology,* 6, 271-307.

Miller, W. B. (1978). The intendedness and wantedness of the first child. In W. B. Miller, L. F. Newman (Eds.), *The first child and family formation.* Chapel Hill, Carolina Population Center, 209-243.

Miller, W. B. (1983). Chance, choice, and the future of reproduction. *American Psychologist,* 38, 1198-1205.

Miller, W. B., Godwin, R. K. (1977). *Psyche and demos.* New York, Oxford University Press.

Mohr, J. C. (1978). *Abortion in America: The origins and evolution of national policy. 1800-1900.* New York, Oxford University Press.

Moore, E. C.(1974). *International inventory of information on induced abortion.* New York, International Institute for the Study of Human Reproduction, Columbia University.

Munson, M. L. (1977). Wanted and unwanted births reported by mothers 15-44 years of age: United States, 1973. *Advance data from vital and health statistics of the National Center for Health Statistics,* 10 August, 1977, No. 9.

Müllner, J., Ruisel, I., Farkaš, G. (1980). *Questionnaire to measure anxiety and anxiousness.* (In Czech.) Bratislava, Psychodiagnostika.

Muramatsu, M. (1974). The Japanese experience. In H. P. David (Ed.), *Abortion Research: International Experience.* Lexington, Mass., Lexington Books, 133-136.

Myhrman, A. (1977). The mother-child project in Northern Finland: Relationship between family migration and child development at school age studied in a sociomedical risk group. *Nordic Council Arctic Medical Research Report,* 20, 43.

Myhrman, A. (1982). Undesired pregnancy and children's life circumstances. In *Yearbook of Population Research in Finland,* Helsinki, Vaestöliitto, 20, 68-82.

Myhrman, A. (1985). *The Northern Finland study of unwantedness.* A paper presented at the International workshop on longitudinal studies of "Unwanted children". Oulu, Finland.

Myhrman, A. (1986a). Sex of previous children and desirability of the next child: A follow-up study of unwanted children. In *Yearbook of Population Research in Finland.* Helsinki, The Population Research Institute, 24, 54-59.

Myhrman, A. (1986b). Longitudinal studies on unwanted children. *Scandinavian Journal of Social Medicine,* 14, 57-59.

Myhrman, A., Seitamo, I., Forsius, H. (1984). The effects of unwanted pregnancy on child development: A follow-up study of boys and girls at the age of sixteen. In *Proceedings of the Third International Conference on System Science in Health Care.* Berlin, Springer, 600-603.

Nazer, I. R. (Ed.) (1972). *Induced abortion: A hazard to public health?* Beirut, International Planned Parenthood Federation.

Nebinger, A. (1870). *Criminal abortion: Its extent and prevention.* Philadelphia, Collins.

138

Okpaku, S. O. (1982). The unwanted child and mental illness: A brief selective review. *International Journal of Family Therapy,* 4, 107-113.

Omran, A. R. (1972). Epidemiological and sociological aspects of abortion. In I. R. Nazer (Ed.), *Induced abortion: A hazard to public health?* Beirut, International Planned Parenthood Federation.

Oppitz, G. (1984). *Child or consumption?* (In German.) Boppard, Boldt.

Osborn, F. (1963). Excess and unwanted fertility. *Eugenics Quarterly,* 10, 59-72.

Pohlman, E. W. (1965). "Wanted" and "unwanted": Toward less ambiguous definition. *Eugenics Quarterly,* 12, 19-27.

Pohlman, E. W. (1967). Unwanted conceptions: Research on undersirable consequences. *Eugenics Quarterly,* 14, 143-154.

Pohlman, E. W. (1969). *The psychology of birth planning.* Cambridge, Mass. Schenkman.

Pohlman, E. W. (1970). Childlessness. Intentional and unintentional. *Journal of Mental and Nervous Diseases,* 151, 2-12.

Pohlman, E. W. (1971). The child born after denial of abortion requests. In S. H. Newman, M. B. Beck, S. Levit (Eds.), *Abortion obtained and denied: Research approaches.* New York, The Population Council, 59-74.

Potts, M. D. (1970). Termination of pregnancy. *British Medical Bulletin,* 26, 65-71.

Potts, M. (1971). Impact of English abortion laws on the practice of medicine. In A. J. Sobrero, R. M. Harvey (Eds.), *Advances in planned parenthood.* Vol. 6, Amsterdam, Excerpta Medica, 145-157.

Potts, M., Diggory, P., Peel, J. (1977). *Abortion.* Cambridge, Cambridge University Press.

Pratt, W. F., Mosher, W. D., Bachrach, C. A., Horn, M. C. (1984). Understanding U.S. fertility: Findings from the national survey of family growth. Cycle III. *Population Bulletin,* 39, No. 5.

Rabin, A. I., Haworth, M. R. (1960). *Projective techniques with children,* New York, Grune and Stratton.

Rainwater, L. (1960). *And the poor get children.* Chicago, Quadrangle.

Rantakallio, P. (1969). Groups at risk in low birth weight infants and perinatal mortality. *Acta Paediatrica Scandinavica,* Supplement 193.

Rantakallio, P. (1974). The unwanted child. *Acta Universitatis Oulu,* Series D Medica, No. 8. Obstetrica et Gynaecologica, No. 3.

Rantakallio, P. (1985). *Unwanted Children. The Northern Finland birth cohort. A longitudinal study.* Paper presented at the First International Workshop on Longitudinal Studies of Unwanted Children. Oulu, Finland.

Rantakallio, P., Myhrman, A. (1980). The child and family eight years after undesired conception. *Scandinavian Journal of Social Medicine,* 8, 81-87.

Rasmussen, N. Kr. (1983). *Abortion — one choice?* (In Danish.) Copenhagen, FADL.

Reiterman, C. (1971). Unwanted Children. In C. Reiterman (Ed.), *Abortion and the unwanted child.* The Californian Committee on Therapeutic Abortion. New York, Springer, 115-120.

Rohner, R. P. (1980). *Handbook for the study of parental acceptance and rejection.* Storrs, The University of Connecticut.

Rohner, R. P. (1986). *The Warmth Dimension.* Beverly Hills, Sage Publications.

Rohner, R. P., Rohner, E. C. (1980). Worldwide tests of parental acceptance-rejection theory. *Behavior Science Research,* 15, 1-22.

Ruisel, I., Müllner, J. (1982). *DOPEN.* (In Czech.) Bratislava, Psychodiagnostika.

Ryder, N. (1973). Contraceptive failure in the United States. *Family Planning Perspectives,* 5, 133-142.

Ryder, N. B., Westoff, C. F. (1971). *Reproduction in the United States.* Princeton, Princeton University Press.

Sanger, M. (1916). Speech given at Hotel Brevoort, New York City, 17 January. Cited in M. Gray: *Margaret Sanger,* New York, Marek, 1979, p. 117.

Schaefer, E. S. (1965). Children's report of parental behavior: An inventory. *Child Development,* 36, 413-424.

Schaefer, E. S., Bell, R. Q. (1958). Development of a parental attitude research instrument. *Child Development,* 29, 339-351.

Schludermann, E., Schludermann, S. (1970). Replicability of factors in Children's Report of Parental Behavior (CRPBI). *Journal of Psychology,* 78, 239-246.

Schulte, W. et al. (1969). *Unerwünschte Schwangerschaft.* Stuttgart, G. Thieme.

Schüller, V., Dytrych, Z., Matějček, Z. (1976). Stability of family and educational environment in families with unwanted children. (In Czech.) *Demografie,* 18, 324-331.

Schüller, V., Stupková, E. (1967). Social questions of pregnancy interruption and possibilities of their study. (In Czech.) *Demografie,* 9, 216-220.

Schüller, V., Stupková, E. (1970). Legal abortion and the possibilities of studying its psychosocial consequences. In H. P. David et al. (Eds.), *Transnational studies in family planning.* Budapest, September, 1969. Washington, American Institutes of Research, 12-14.

139

Schüller, V., Stupková, E. (1972). The "unwanted child" in the family. *International Mental Health Research Newsletter,* 14, 2, 6-11, 14-18.

Schüller, V., Stupková, E. (1973). Unwanted child in the family. (In Czech.) *Demografie,* 15, 40-45, 121-129.

Simms, M., Hindell, K. (1971). *Abortion law reformed.* London, Owen.

Simpson, J. Y. (1872). *Clinical lectures of the diseases of women.* Edinburgh, Clark.

Spielberger, C. D., Gursuch, R. L., Lushene, R. E. (1970). *Manual for the State-Trait Anxiety Inventory.* Palo Alto, Consulting Psychologist Press.

Stampar, D. (1973). Outcome of pregnancy in women whose requests for legal abortion have been denied. *Studies in Family Planning,* 4, 267-269.

Stepan, J. (Ed.) (1979). *Survey of laws on fertility control.* New York, United Nations Fund for Population Activities.

Stephenson, J. (1975). *Women in Nazi society.* New York, Barnes and Noble.

Šturma, J., Müller, Č. (1970). To the question of unwanted pregnancies. (In Czech.) *Československá gynekologie,* 35, 35-37.

Taussig, F. (1936). *Abortion — spontaneous and induced: Medical and social aspects.* St. Louis, Mosby.

Tietze, C., Henshaw, S. K. (1986). *Induced abortion: A world review 1986.* New York, Alan Guttmacher Institute.

Wechsler, D. (1955). *Wechsler Intelligence Scale for Children. Manual.* New York, Psychological Corporation.

Werner, N. K., Kirschner, L. G. (1972). Unwanted pregnancies. In N. Morris (Ed.), *Psychosomatic medicine in obstetrics and gynaecology. Third International Congress. London, 1971.* Basel, S. Karger, 527-530.

Westoff, C. F. (1981). The decline in unwanted fertility. *Family Planning Perspectives,* 13, 70-72.

World Health Organization (1971). *Abortion laws: A survey of current world legislation.* Geneva.

Zemlic, M. J., Watson, R. J. (1953). Maternal attitudes of acceptance and rejection during and after pregnancy. *American Journal of Orthopsychiatry,* 23, 570-584.

Ždímalová, M., Kopečný, J., Novák, A. (1970). Follow-up of women whose application for pregnancy interruption was denied. (In Czech.) *Československá gynekologie,* 35, 338.

Subject Index

142